Self Improvement
through a new approach to
Evolution

Self Improvement
through a new approach to
Evolution

by Shaun Johnston

Illustrations by the author

VOLVED
ELF
PUBLISHING

Self Improvement Through a New Approach to Evolution
by Shaun Johnston
Illustrations and cover art by the author

Published by
Evolved Self Publishing
www.evolvedself.com

Evolved Self Publishing is an imprint of
Shaun Johnston Design Ltd

ISBN: 0-9779470-3-3

This book is dedicated
to the memory of

Alfred Wallace
1823-1913

Wallace was the first person to submit the idea of
natural selection for publication.

"That's true!"

CHARLES DARWIN

But a few years later Wallace abandoned his own theory,
because ***it could not account for human evolution***.

This book takes up
Wallace's argument

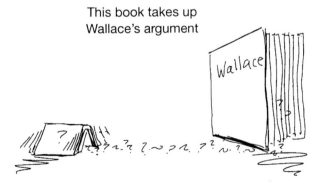

Helping the modern self...

... tap into the powers behind the natural world

Contents

Introduction to a new self

"What's wrong with our old self?"

What's wrong is, our conscious self, with all its feelings and emotions, is not one self, it's lots of selfs, all jumbled together. Some come from hundreds of years ago, others come from thousands of years ago. We've no idea how it all works. We're just coasting, hoping it won't fall apart.

How has the conscious self got to where it is today?

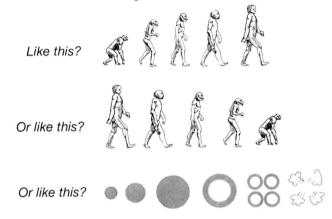

Like this?

Or like this?

Or like this?

No one knows. We don't know what the conscious self looks like, how to measure it, even what's it's made of. We don't even know how to think about it. Until we figure that out, we won't know how to fix it.

"So how can we go about making a better self"

● **By coming up with a new way of thinking** about the conscious self, so we can make sense of it, and figure out how to fix it.

● **Once we know how to fix it** we can make it better, better than ever.

That's what this book is about. It's a set of three handbooks for people looking for new approaches to the self, and new ways to improve it.

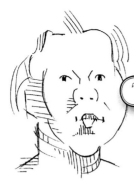

"Can science tell us what we want to know about the self?"

No. First science has to know what something is made of.
But science doesn't know what consciousness is made of. So
it can't tell us anything about it.

Instead of the question, **"What is the self made of?"** we'll be
better off starting with a different question.

Sometimes, when you want to fix something, it helps to know
how it was made. So let's begin by asking, **"How was the self
made?"**

"OK, how was the self made?"

The answer is, **Evolution!** Our conscious self evolved along
with the rest of us.

Evolution is the right kind of answer. It can explain why we're
so creative.

Evolution is creative, physics isn't.

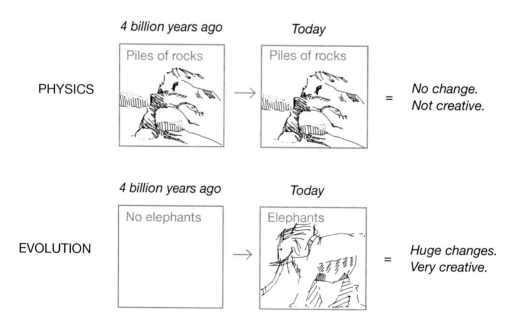

So evolution is where we should look for how the self was made.

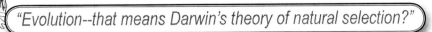

"Evolution--that means Darwin's theory of natural selection?"

Not so fast. When Darwin's theory has been applied to human beings the results have been bad:

- **Social Darwinism** (bad).

- **Eugenics** (bad).

Sorry —

CHARLES DARWIN

"What's wrong with natural selection?"

It's just more physics. Here's how it goes:

> *"Every so often, random errors occur in our genes. If these errors help us survive long enough to reproduce they'll survive too, at the expense of the molecules they replace, until there's enough of these changed genes to define a new species."*

This is all about random changes to molecules (genes), about those random changes getting mechanically sorted, resulting in a different selection of genes than those we started with. It's about nothing but molecules. That may be OK as physics, but what it says about the self is terrible.

What kind of genes will it select for? Genes that make you:

- **Aggressive**, doing whatever makes you most competitive.

- **Promiscuous**, doing whatever makes you have most children.

- **A bully** of other people's children, so your children survive to pass on your genes.

A monster!

But we're not all like this. So we couldn't have evolved just through natural selection. Anyway, that process couldn't generate conscious selfs. It would just make different chemicals.

There is. It's called "**Lamarckism**" after a biologists called "Lamarck," just as "Darwinism" is named after Charles Darwin. And it's about the self, and the self helping itself. It might be just what we're looking for.

Problem is, it's very out of date. There's nothing in it about the genome.

The genome

Our complete genetic code, written out in one long string.

This information actually comes in long molecules, the chromosomes. We've 46 of them in each cell in our bodies.

The atoms that make up chromosomes arrange themselves in a double spiral, like the drawing at left.

In this book, when you see this double spiral, it stands for all our genetic code, that's almost everything needed to code for what turns a single cell into a full human being.

A genome is one long thread that codes for a living creature. You could call it a "**living filament**"—see below:

Charles Darwin's grandfather, Erasmus Darwin, was one of the first people to come up with a theory of evolution. "Couldn't all warm-blood-ied creatures have come from **one living filament**," he wondered. It's this "living filament" that invents new organs, he said, that makes us intelligent, and helps us adjust to the environment. In fact, couldn't all living creatures, he supposed, have come from filaments like that?

His "**living filament**" is like what we now call the genome. So, long before Charles Darwin came up with natural selection, his grandfather imagined evolution being driven by something like the genome.

Can we build on his idea? Can we come up with a new theory of evolution by joining his idea to what we know about the genome today?

Let's try.

Rethinking evolution from scratch

What do we know, that we want to account for?

- We know we have a thinking conscious self.

- We know we experience feelings.

- We know we're creative.

What else do we know?

- We know all the information needed to grow a person from a single cell to an adult human being lies in the genome.

Now— let's be creative!

Let's figure out how we got made.

To make something as complicated as a human being, starting from a single cell, wouldn't you have to be intelligent yourself?

> *"We don't make our brains. The genome makes them. Shouldn't whatever makes us be at least as intelligent as we are? In fact, it must be a lot smarter. I've no idea how to make a brain like mine, have you?"*

THE AUTHOR

Let's supose that, if the genome can make intelligent conscious human beings with selfs, it's intelligent too. After all, we'd have to be intelligent to do something creative like that.

Thinks...

But, if so...

"What's the genome going to use for a brain?"

For us to think we have to have a brain. Where's the "brain" for a genome's thinking?

It must be the genome itself, the molecules it's made of. That's all there is to it.

Genome's intelligence ————— Thinks...

Genome's brain—itself! —————

"How would that work?"

Look at what happens when one of us thinks. We send messages to our brain cells telling them to make our muscles move. In us, thinking works by us making changes in our brain.

If the genome's thinking works like ours then, as the genome thinks, it's going to make changes in the stuff it's made of—genes.

"But isn't that how evolution works, by making changes in genes?"

That's right. **We've come up with a new theory of evolution**:

It says **evolution works by the genome thinking**, which changes the genes it's made of. The genome can literally "dream up" new species, just by thinking them, as people dream up stories or new fashions.

Thinks... *"What kind of creature shall I dream up today?"*

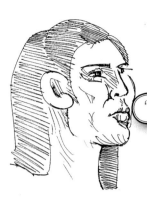

> *"Then, we're nothing but a thought the genome once had?"*

No, we're more than that. Don't forget, we're where the genome lives. There's one in every cell in our body. It depends on us for its existence, completely.

We're like planetary rovers the genome sends out to report back what the surface of the Earth is like.

A self-propelled Earth rover

We're its explorers. We're very important to it. So it's going to make us the very best creatures it can.

> *"We're just a machine?"*

> *"Which one of us is the real human being?"*

That's up to you. You can choose. Are you a machine? Or a body with a conscious thinking self?

You're a machine?
OK, then you can have evolved mechanically, your genes getting altered at random and then getting sorted for their survival value through mutation and natural selection.

Or, you have a conscious thinking self?
Then evolution takes place in a world where conscious thinking selves can exist. Those selves can drive evolution—just look at how we've changed the environment of every living creature! You'll need a theory that takes other conscious thinking selves into account.

Let's make that choice a little clearer:

The Natural Selection Self

First, your genes suffer random damage.

Then there's selection for how well those genes make sure you survive, reproduce and pass on your genes, instead of someone else's.

The genes selected for by this process would make you:

- **Aggressive.** Your ancestors always over-came the competition.

- **Promiscuous.** Your ancestors always had the most young.

- **A bully.** Your ancestors always made sure their young got to survive to reproduce in the next generation.

That's how we'd all be if we'd evolved through natural selection and survival of the fittest.

PROFESSOR SAYS: How's natural selection supposed to work? By selecting for creatures better adapted to their environment.

But that's not enough. Of course they have to be adapted to their environment, or else they couldn't stay alive.

The real question is, why are they—and we!—so much more than just "adapted"? Natural selection can't account for that.

Example: elephants and giraffes live in the same environment. If all that mattered was being adapted they'd look the same, perfectly adapted to the same environment. Why are they actually so different, with such distinct personalities?

And where did the human self come from? There's nothing like the human self in the environment. Calling it an adaptation tells you nothing about it.

What's needed to account for evolution? Obviously more than just becoming adapted. So there must be something else involved in evolution besides natural selection.

The Self we want to account for

We're looking for a theory that can account for how we really are:

- **Thoughtful**, interested in the well-being of others, their children, even other species.

- **Creative**, something natural selection and physics can't account for.

- **Conscious**, free to make up our own minds, able to put our conscious thoughts into practice. We're not just robots created by physics.

Unless our theory can account for all that, it won't help us find ways of making ourselves more like that: more thoughtfull and considerate of one another, more creative, more fully conscious.

What shall we put in here?

Where should we look for clues to the self? There's only three places. There's (1) the physical world, **the environment**, but that doesn't have anything like consciousness in it.

There's (2) **individual living creatures**. But they can't make new selfs, they don't survive from one generation to the next.

That leaves (3) **the genome**. The genome's existed continuously for 4 billion years, copying itself over and over again. That's the only place left to look for a self. That must be it!

Could the genome have a self, and be creative and intelligent? Well, we have selfs, we're creative and intelligent, so other living creatures could be too. Why not the genome? It's alive, isn't it?

> *"Must either the 'intelligent genome' theory or natural selection be true? Probably neither theory is completely true or false. You're probably better off believing each one where it applies.*
>
> *"In the case of the 'intelligent genome' theory, it applies when you're thinking about creativity and the self. Natural selection can't help you there."*

THE AUTHOR

The genome wakes!

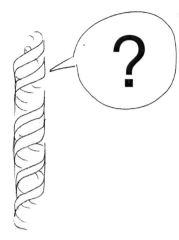

Imagine you're a genome.

Imagine waking up to find you're intelligent.

You're actually buried inside the cells of living creatures. But, as you think, your thoughts change those living creatures into new species. These species end up being little automated Earth rovers that roam the world for you.

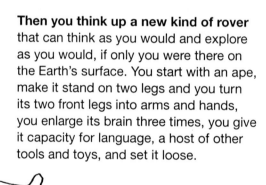

You eventually get so good at building these rovers you figure out how to build into them some of your own intelligence.

Then you think up a new kind of rover that can think as you would and explore as you would, if only you were there on the Earth's surface. You start with an ape, make it stand on two legs and you turn its two front legs into arms and hands, you enlarge its brain three times, you give it capacity for language, a host of other tools and toys, and set it loose.

That's us. That's why we're so different from other animals. We're a new model, the first in a new line, the smartest Earth rovers yet. We were such a good design we spread over the whole planet, from the poles to the Equator.

How did the genome equip us for our mission? How can we use those gifts for self improvement?

What's in this book

Handbook 1

Embracing the gifts

The genome equips its creatures with wonderful gifts. Here's how to make the most of the gifts given to our species.

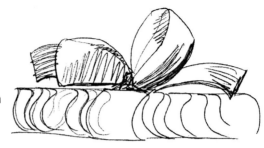

Handbook 2

Harnessing the processes

What is unique about the human species? The genome gave us, and us alone, keys to the technologies needed to grow and maintain a living creature. Learn how our ancestors harnessed those technologies to create civilization, and how we can apply these technologies to enhance our own thinking.

Handbook 3

Finding new meaning

That we evolved is a new and revolutionary idea. What does it tell us about our nature? What new possibilities does it open up? What does it tell us about meaning in life? We're only at the very beginning of a new chapter in human evolution.

For references and sources see "Save Our Selves from Science Gone Wrong" by Shaun Johnston, published by Evolved Self Publishing in 2008.

1
Handbook

Embracing the gifts

What goes into making up a self? *Consciousness and thinking. Dreaming. Our senses. Feelings and meanings. Personality. Creeativity. All our varied mental and physical capabilities.*

Chapter by chapter, this handbook traces the origin of each of these talents to gifts bestowed on us by the genome. Suggestions follow for how we can harness these gifts to enhance our own self.

Have a problem to tackle? Don't assume you're limited to just the talents we'd have if we evolved through natural selection. Those talents would merely make us "adapted to the environment."

Don't tie your self down by assuming
you're merely "adapted."

Instead, say to yourself, "I'm the product of the genome, a genius of boundless engineering talent. I am a workshop packed with ingenious tools. I'll select from those tools to create a solution for myself."

Gifts accounted for in this Handbook:

Capabilities of our bodies
Emotions, sense of humor
Skills built into us
Conscious attention
Thinking as meanings evolving
Dreaming and consciousness
Personality

CHAPTER 1

Gift 1:
How we come equipped

In the introduction I suggested we're creatures the genome just thought up.

What for? To be its "Earth rovers," scouts the genome sends out to explore the Earth's surface on its behalf.

How well-equipped are we for our mission? Wonderfully. Let's look at capabilities the genome's built into us.

The genome applies its genius for engineering far and wide. Other species give us wonderful illustrations of how great its engineering is.

- **A spider** is a master engineer. It begins by placing anchor points sometimes several feet apart, as if it had already visualized the completed web. It builds its web out of a number of different glues and threads, some as strong as any material we know how to make.

- **Ants have a talent for architecture.** They make elaborate nests that are, in effect, entire cities, complex in structure and thousands of times as big as a single ant.

- **Beavers** come equipped with teeth and jaws that can chop through trees several inches thick. Then they're able to use these trees to construct dams.

- **A new-born foal.** Until a few moments ago the foal experienced only the darkness and weightless support of the inside of the womb. Yet within minutes of being born it can balance itself on its spindly legs against gravity and walk and then canter. And almost immediately it learns to focus its attention on something it's never seen before—its mother.

Beaver skull. A nice piece of engineering

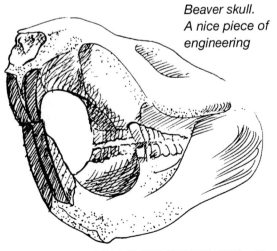

Were we left out when these wonderful gifts were handed around? I don't think so.

Take even the simplest of our capabilities:

reflexes

If I run near the edge of a cliff, my body will instinctively pull me away—it doesn't give me any choice in the matter.

It's surprisingly smart. I have no head for heights and can't stand near the edge of a floor suspended over an empty space. But if there's a glass window rising from floor to ceiling at the edge I can go up to that edge with no problem, even if I can't see my reflection, even though there's no evidence of the glass except me knowing it's there. My body will trust my knowing about the glass.

Even a simple reflex action can pack a lot of smarts.

Now take the capabilities behind our basic housekeeping

My body knows how to do things like initiate urinating. I've no idea how it does that, I just tell it to and it unlocks all the necessary valves and levers, then afterwards closes them up again. As for breathing and adjusting heart beat, I don't ever have to think about them.

All this happens so unobtrusively it's hard to appreciate how much engineering's gone into them.

Can even love and affection be built in us by the genome?

Take dogs. Have you experienced a dog's passionate affection and exquisite sensitivity to what you say and do? Don't they seem to have a self quite like ours? That sensitivity evolved in dogs as they got used to living with humans. It's not part of the nature of wolves, dogs' near relative. When dogs were compared to chimpanzees and wolves, only dogs showed any of this sensitivity.

It appears at full strength even in puppies raised with no human contact at all. It's part of the nature they're born with, engineered into them by the genome.

Are our feelings going to be any different?.

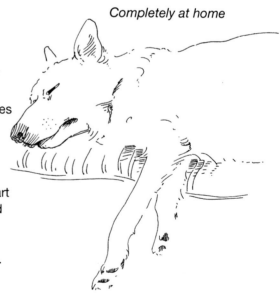

Completely at home

How about our elaborate
sense of humor?

We seem to have a **sense of fun** like that of kittens or sea otters playing. But we seem to need to signal that we "get" jokes by laughing. Is that something we invented, or did we get it from the genome?

What is a laugh? Where does it come from? If you listen to it carefully, laughter has a very primitive sound. It starts with a filling of the lungs, and then a series of sharp barks. The first one is high-pitched. Then as the lungs empty, the pitch of the sound lowers, until breath must be drawn once more, and the pitch of the laugh starts high once more. Isn't it like the sound of sea lions calling? Like the sound dinosaurs might have made? Could the sounds of laughter actually come from an earlier stage in our evolution?

I like to think, when we're tickled, we recapture a faint memory of how our reptile-like ancestors felt. To them, vibrations on the ground, sensed through what would become the palms of our hands and feet, and impacts on their vulnerable flanks—our ribs—would be warnings of danger. These are just the places where we are most ticklish, that we respond to with the sinuous wriggling of a lizard, while making curious cries and feeling a desperate urge to escape. We're simultaneously entertained and angry. And we laugh.

When you find yourself laughing like this, do you feel in control? I don't. I feel curiously out of control, as if I have been taken over by a quite primitive behavior.

I like to think that, when the genome wanted to give us some new expressions to signal humor, it drew on some old and obsolete reptilian cries that lay dormant in our nature. Why bother to create new cries when these old cries would do? That's the mark of a master engineer.

Do you see a hint of a smile?

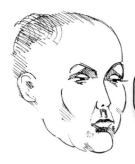

"What problems can I solve with these gifts? How about feeling sad?"

Coping with Sadness

Laughing may be just a simple trick of genetic engineering but when we're sad all we want to do is laugh. Can laughing itself banish the blues? At a workshop I attended the leader broke the ice by tapping into this part of our engineering. He had us all jump up and down like bears while booming in a very deep voice. We all broke out into real laughter. It was a great tension-releaser.

All self help gurus agree, laughter is wonderful medicine, a great mood enhancer. Just acting out laughing can help make us happy.

How about being lonely?"

Loneliness

You can be among people yet feel lonely. You need to engage them somehow.

Suggestion: place your faith in the abundant talents the genome builds into us, just waiting to be developed. Develop a skill you can practice in public, such as juggling. Other people will be drawn to you and want to talk about what you're doing.

How can such extraordinary creatures as we are not be a delight to each other? Perhaps because we undervalue ourselves, not realizing how amazing we are, not expecting enough of ourselves and each other, not taking the trouble to make the most of the extraordinary resources the genome built into us.

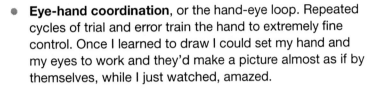
How about learning a new skill?"

Talents like drawing often involve two skills. We find the genome's built into us a pair of skills that complement each other. One lies in the doing, the other lies in the appreciating of what we've done.

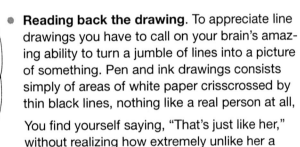

- **Eye-hand coordination**, or the hand-eye loop. Repeated cycles of trial and error train the hand to extremely fine control. Once I learned to draw I could set my hand and my eyes to work and they'd make a picture almost as if by themselves, while I just watched, amazed.

- **Reading back the drawing**. To appreciate line drawings you have to call on your brain's amazing ability to turn a jumble of lines into a picture of something. Pen and ink drawings consists simply of areas of white paper crisscrossed by thin black lines, nothing like a real person at all,

  You find yourself saying, "That's just like her," without realizing how extremely unlike her a bunch of black lines on paper actually is.

  This is not something you can take for granted. Kittens brought up so they saw lines only at one particular angle never got to "see" lines at other angles. They never developed the mental machinery needed for detecting lines at any other angle.

"I learned to draw late in life, in my forties. To make up for lost time, I wanted to learn as quickly as possible. I looked for machinery in me that would give me good feedback on how I was doing.

"I knew we have special centers in the brain dedicated to recognizing faces and expressions, so when you draw faces it's very obvious whether you succeeded or not. I enlarged line drawings of faces four times and traced over them for hours at a time. With a couple of years' practice I learned to draw, and I still get a lot of pleasure out of it."

Sometimes I test the limits of our line-reading machinery by seeing how far I can distort my drawings before the brain loses the ability to recognize what it's a drawing of.

Can you see a line of trees here, with clouds to the right?

Or I see what minimal set of lines the brain can still read. It's extraordinary how we can make sense of the simplest wiggle.

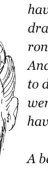

PROFESSOR SAYS: *These talents couldn't have evolved by natural selection. Line drawing wasn't much use in "the environment" until we had pen and paper. And there couldn't have been much need to decipher line drawings, when there weren't any! So how could skills like this have evolved?*

A better explanation is, they're part of the bounty the genome designed into us, to make us better scouts.

Look in the phone book and you get the impression that humans come with a fixed set of skills, like those of a plumber or an electrician. In fact, we come with a huge range of gifts that blend into one another to give us an almost unlimited ability to solve our own problems.

CHAPTER 2

Gift 2:
Attention—you can make it priceless

Everyone's birthright:
Attention worth $15 million

Advertisers know how much your attention's worth. For each 30 seconds of it they'll pay around 3 cents. Over a lifetime that amounts to $15 million.

They'll pay that much because they know that what enters your attention will determine how you think, feel and behave.

Shouldn't your attention be worth at least as much to you as it is to them?

Our attention is the unloading dock for what gets added to our self. It literally shapes our future selfs. Whatever we pay attention to today will become the resources available to us for self improvement tomorrow.

When you retire, paying attention may be the only form of entertainment you can afford. It's priceless.

What goes into paying attention?
From natural selection you wouldn't expect very much: just a few simple scanning devices to prevent you bumping into things and help you identify food and members of the opposite sex, and reflexes to automatically turn those scanning devices towards or away from whatever looks promising or threatening.

But in fact you've a set of instruments so fantastic it leaves human technology, even human imagination, far behind, plus the ability to direct those instruments however you want to enrich your conscious experience.

Attention the natural-selection way would be just a passive receiving of impressions. The intelligent-genome way is paying attention consciously.

Attention depends on a whole lot of senses we're usually not aware of.

Unless you're a trapeze artist!

Then you'd have to be piercingly aware of your physical self, swinging and spinning in thin air, targeted at a precise alignment in space and time with another swinging body. Then you know very well how much you're depending on some very sophisticated equipment.

● First, the surface of your brain carries at least two maps of your body complete with arms and hands and fingers, legs and toes, your head with eyes and lips, all connected and all pretty much in the right place.

● Then, as well as senses of pain and touch, we've special senses telling us how our joints are bent. Pressure on our feet tells us if we're standing on terra firma. All this information gets referred to the two maps to tell us where all the parts of our bodies are in relation to each other, and where they're being touched or how we should move them in relation to each other.

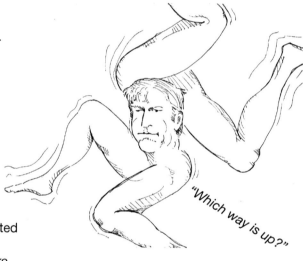

"Which way is up?"

● And there's apparatus associated with our ears that tells us how we're oriented in space, if we're spinning, and how we're spinning, in all three dimensions.

THE AUTHOR

"I had vivid proof of the power and sensitivity of this apparatus when I had an infection of the inner ear that disrupted it.

"I lost all sense of my location in space. The slightest movement of my head induced violent nausea. I could only crawl."

> *"**These hidden senses** are essential to the working of the senses we do pay attention with. Even when I'd mostly recovered from my organ of balance being infected my vision remained distorted—if I tracked cars as they passed by they jumped about as if on elastic cords. So vision is precisely synchronized with exquisitely-engineered gyroscopes in our heads, just as in NASA's Moon rovers.*
>
> *"We also use the bits of us we can see out of the corners of our eyes to connect what our internal senses tell us with everything else we can see outside, to put our selfs 'in the picture.'"*

THE AUTHOR

How can we tell where all the bits of us are in space? Sometimes I close my eyes and try to position the tips of the index fingers of my two hands so they're just touching. Doesn't matter if I do this behind my back, over my head, or between my legs, my two fingertips usually turn out to be within an inch of each other. For me to do that, all the joints involved have to talk together, telling each other how much they're bent. How many joints are there between the finger tips on the two hands? At least a dozen.

Hearing

The engineering behind hearing seems crackpot. It's a tiny fringe of hairs like the string edging a rug but getting shorter from one end to the other and then coiled up into a spiral. Yet we can hear an amazing range of loud and soft, high and low.

We can even place sounds in space around us.

> *"Sometimes I entertain myself by testing this. In a roomful of people I close my eyes, and focus them blindly on where people's voices seem to be coming from. When I open my eyes I can tell how close the judgments of ears and eyes are. Usually, very close. Our senses work very closely together."*

Sight

Want assurance you are wonderful? You needn't rely on compliments. Look no farther than the lens in your own eye. It's alive, it has to be equipped with oxygen, yet it appears perfectly transparent.

It grows in layers that perfectly correct for the color fringing you get when you look through glass lenses.

As if that wasn't enough, you got not one eye but two! Go into a garden and close one eye. All the vegetation will flatten into a single confused layer. Twigs and leaves will merge together into a flat carpet. Open both eyes and all those details spring forth distinct, uniquely located in space. Walk around the garden, and your 3D vision shows you all the plants, every leaf, every twig, distinct and isolated in space, updating instantly—not the slightest delay.

If you've any experience with computer graphic software you've got to be in awe of how much computing power we've got built into us, to pick out each leaf and twig in 3D in a garden like this.

Just these few examples show how much technology the genome has at its disposal, to lavish on its creatures.

We're equipped way beyond what you'd need for mere survival, which is all natural selection would care about.

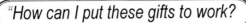

"How can I put these gifts to work?"

Let's look at ways we can get $15 millions-worth of value, or more, by consciously directing this fantastic equipment.

Tips on how to pay attention

What's the ultimate freedom?

For me, being able to direct my attention is the ultimate freedom. I can look wherever I want. I'm the director of my own movie, at every instant.

Here are some ways I've learned to creatively direct my attention:

- **Vary how narrowly you focus your attention.**
  You can take in your surroundings in a broad sweep, or focus narrowly on a detail. You can focus intently on a situation taking place far away in the distance, then switch to another distant scene. You can actively sample your surroundings far and wide, without moving.

- **Change what you're paying most attention to.**
  For example, you might shift your attention from people's movements to the color of their clothes. From seeing to hearing. You might pay attention to a combination of hearing and touching. Or take in impressions from all your senses at once, for example in a busy market. Then focus just on people, turning towards them to focus on them one after another.

- **Focus on particular aspects of things.**
  You might decide to focus your attention on how differently women and men react in a situation, for example. Of course, we do this kind of thing all the time, but if you're bored you do it deliberately, just for fun.

- **No filter at all—the vacation experience.**
  I can switch off most of my filtering at will, and see my surroundings freshly. It's delightful, with a little of the feeling of ecstasy about it. One way to induce this when you're out walking somewhere interesting is to turn around, maybe even slowly walk back the way you came. Even simple curiosity—"what's next?"—can narrow your focus. Looking backwards over territory you've already traversed can disable curiosity, leaving you free to experience awareness itself.

Vision	It's all under your control,
Smell	every moment.
Taste	
Hearing	Training your attention
Touch	can be hugely rewarding.
Memory	

THE AUTHOR

"Being a photographer and painter has given me two different ways of looking at things. One way is the regular way, looking at things for what they're for—a table, a chair, a window, a carpet. But I can switch at will to a different way of seeing, looking at the same things for the pictures they make, in terms of shapes, textures and colors."

You can train yourself to do this by using an artist's aid, a piece of card with a rectangular hole cut in it. When you view the world through the hole, it turns into pictures. That helps you to find pictures around you.

Another way to switch from things-seeing to picture-seeing is to close one eye. Disabling 3D vision emphasizes how things look, as flat pictures.

"When I'm driving on a very quiet country road I'll slow down, lean forward until my nose is almost touching the windscreen, and close one eye. Suddenly the view in front of me is transformed into a stream of pictures. I see one fabulous photo, then it melts, then I see another one. The experience is similar to watching Cinerama. Open both eyes, and the pictorial aspect vanishes, and I'm back in the "real" world. A delightful experience either way."

"Sometimes I experiment with vision just to see what it can do. For example, I'll try to stitch together a panorama of my surroundings in my mind's eye by slowly turning around. I thought that would be easy, but it's surprisingly difficult. The genome forgot to equip us with the ability to stitch together a continuous 360 degree image.

"That shows that anything our senses can do doesn't happen just because we've eyes and ears. Each talent had to be specially built into us."

The present moment
How long is "the present moment"?

"I know my present moment doesn't extend to the ten minutes it takes a Datura flower to open. I can string together memories of how a flower looks along the way, but I can't experience the entire opening as a single process.

THE AUTHOR

"I'd say my present moment is no more than a second or two. Maybe when we watch diving or skating we can start a new present moment and extend it to 3 or 4 seconds, but I think that's about the limit."

The present moment may be short, but it's uniquely precious. In our present moment, data is uncompressed, raw, available for all kinds of mental play.

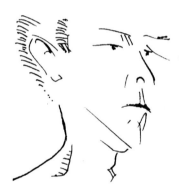

"As an amateur caricaturist, I experience this directly. At a party, as people swirl by me, in a second or so I can collapse each face in my imagination into a caricature. But when I recall a face from memory, I can't reduce it to caricature. Once stored in memory, that data's been reduced, compressed, "cooked." I can't "un-cook" it and then "re-cook" it some other way."

Subject matter is better "uncooked"

The problem with most media is the content comes pre-cooked. Either it's been edited as it passed through someone else's attention or it comes out of a studio where the free-play of attention has been strictly limited.

Anyway, media automatically place limits on our attention by making us attend to a flat screen in the center of our attention (video or movies) or by playing to a single sense instead of all of them (music, talk shows).

The best that media can offer us pales beside the incredible richness of detail and possibilities the genome equipped us to savor in the uncooked real-life present moment.

"Can I put the attention to practical use?

I used to be a graphic designer. Then I became a writer. But I got bored, so I switched to something really creative. I became a salesman.

The ideal "attention" profession --Sales!
The sales call is one of the most intense present-moment experiences. Think of it; you walk into an unfamiliar office with barely more than a pen and paper in your hand, maybe a brochure or two, and your business card. You meet a complete stranger, you shake hands, sit down facing each other. You may know nothing about this person at all. You're looking very intently at him or her, at the office, at signs on the wall. The opening of a sales call is a flood of impression and information, as if the world were fresh-washed. Everything is very bright.

Your primary tool is your attention. You must be very alert. But you must also be relaxed; very open to the unexpected. You may begin with a prepared pitch, but you'll be looking for any opportunity to deviate from it to shift the engagement in the direction of the other person's interests.

Are you in control of your attention?

Are you actually free to look wherever you want? Or is your attention driven by your brain chemistry? Are you determined by how your brain chemistry directs your attention? Are you really a robot?

You can bet that when I'm a salesman in someone else's office I think I'm in charge of my own attention. I think I'm free to look where I want, I think I'm free to shift the balance from one sense, such as hearing, to another such as sight.

But am I really in control of my own thinking? That's taken up in Handbook 2. For now, let's ask, what does thinking consist of?

PROFESSOR SAYS: You could try to account for all the wonders built into your attention through natural selection. But are you likely to try? I don't think so. All natural selection would lead you to expect from your attention would be just the minimum needed to survive, just "adaptations." Why would you suppose you could do anything creative to make paying attention more enjoyable, as suggested in this chapter?

To expect more from your attention, you have to turn to some other account of how you evolved.

CHAPTER 3

Gift 3:
Thinking as thoughts evolving

How does the genome's Earth rover (each of us) "think"?

Put in quotes like that, "think" means data processing, managing all the zeros and ones, chips, computer systems, that sort of thing, that engineers build into real planetary rovers to run everything.

Of course, in us it really is thinking. But what is thinking?

It's easy for a Darwinist to claim that everything we've looked at so far is really just an adaptation to the environment. But what does that mean? **Why, in a similar environment**, does a spider spin a web and a bee make a hive? Saying that such different and elaborate capabilities are different adaptations to the same environment tells you nothing. Why do those so-called adaptations take such different and creative forms?

The reason is, they're not just adaptations, they're hugely inventive creations of the genome.

We know that because what makes us human beings—thinking, and consciousness—can't arise through natural selection. Here's why—according to science, thinking and consciousness aren't physical, so they can't have any impact on the environment. But if they can't have any impact on the environment they can't make any difference to survival. And if they don't make any difference to survival they can't be selected by natural selection. So thinking and consciousness can't have evolved!

But we know thinking and consciousness did evolve, because we experience them.

Let's start with thinking. How does that work?

> *From the introduction:*
> When the genome thinks, its thoughts make changes in the genes it's made of. The results is new species— something evolving. So evolving involves thinking.

When it made us, the genome built into us some of its own powers, including thinking. Maybe, for us to think, it had to build into us something that could evolve.

Let's suppose, thinking is our thoughts evolving.

Only, it's evolution happening very fast! Imagine the evolution of thoughts taking only seconds instead of hundreds of thousands of years for living species. That's how fast thoughts must evolve in our minds if thinking actually is our thoughts evolving.

Can we use this idea to help our self?

If thinking is evolving, then what we learn about evolution we could apply to improve how we think. You'd simply say to yourself, let's evolve some ideas. You'd come up with some ideas, set them evolving, and see what results.

That's taken up in Handbook 2. For now, take inspiration from the wonders of nature, knowing the inventive power involved in the creation of those wonders lies behind your own thinking, available to enhance it as we learn more about how evolution really works.

If thinking is our thoughts evolving then, more than any other creature we evolve at second hand. We make other creatures—our thoughts— do our evolving for us. We constantly generate new ideas, and let them evolve together. What emerges is a conclusion, corresponding to a new "species," that we can then let loose in the physical world.

How could the process of evolution be built into us to power our thinking except as a gift from the genome?

PROFESSOR SAYS: Why are Darwinists so dead-set against the idea of evolution involving intelligence? That's because they're spooked by Creationists. Creationists claim God creates all living creatures through superhuman intelligence. This so freaks Darwinists out they insist evolution isn't intelligent at all.

Since we're a product of evolution, what does that say about us? That we've no intelligence? On the other hand, if you admit you're intelligent, then how can you claim the process of evolution isn't?

CHAPTER 4

Gift 4:
Feelings, cries and meanings

In a robot, or a creature adapted to its environment by natural selection, the "meaning" of what it did would lie in how it was programmed.

But in us meaning is something we experience. We use meanings to create imaginary universes and imaginary creatures—thoughts—that we set evolving in those universes.

What are meanings?
Are they something vague and abstract? I don't think so. I think they're part of biology.

They're not just some kind of logic. They can flatly contradict one another:

Too many cooks spoil the broth
Many hands make light work

Here are two almost opposite ways of defining strangers:

Those who are not with us are against us.
The enemy of my enemy is my friend

And of course for every philosophy you can find an opposite philosophy. In fact, the point of almost any philosophy seems to be to contradict some other philosophy!

Take baby showers and sales-motivational sessions, for example. They "mean" different things to us. We arrange baby showers one way, to tap into one set of meanings, we arrange sales-motivational sessions another way, to tap into a quite different set of meanings.

So I don't think we're going to find a logical system lying in meanings, waiting to be discovered. Instead, to me they're like creatures. We get to know them through experience. As we get better at identifying them we can start telling heroes from villains, for example, and someone challenging us from someone offering us help.

In this chapter:

- **Meanings seem so abstract**, how could they possibly be "creatures"? Maybe it would help to think of them as having evolved. This chapter begins by imagining a series of steps they could have evolved through.

- **Meanings as tools.** It may seem odd to think of meanings as tools but they certainly can be. I supply some ideas for how to apply them.

1: *We come <u>pre-wired</u> for different kinds of readiness*

Some simple creatures come with fixed networks of nerves. All their behaviors are hard wired—a touch at one spot triggers a particular nerve that make the creature move forward or back. All responses are fixed.

But the way we come wired we can be thrown as a whole into entirely different states. Each makes the body act as a whole, in a distinctive way. Approach and grab, or fight, or run away.

2: *Each state of readiness comes with a feeling*

Isn't that odd? Why do we need feelings? We'd presumably do whatever we were supposed to without needing to feel anything. When we're supposed to panic we'd just run like hell—just being made to run like hell should be enough without us having to feel panicky as well.

Yet we experience a feeling along with each state of readiness we're thrown into.

3: *Each state of readiness also comes with a cry*

Along with each feeling often goes a particular cry, or a sound, like "Aaaah!" or "Ooooh!"

What does something "mean"?

It "means" food or danger, or the state of response that throws us into—approach to eat, or get ready to run away.

But each of those states also goes along with a feeling and a cry.

It's from those feelings and cries we actually identify what things mean to us.

4: *Feelings and cries make up a language*

When we become aggressive, we feel anger, and we growl! OK, we don't actually growl. But we do make certain kinds of sounds.

By mimicking these sounds when we don't actually feel these emotions we can refer to them, and so to the kind of situation that usually causes them. That over there, that's something delicious, "Yumm"! That other thing, that's dangerous, "Uh-oh!" By mimicking our own cries we can tell other people what something "means" to us.

This would give us a basic language of several dozen cries and the corresponding feelings.

5: *Add stories*

I think we get a lot more meanings from what I call "stories." These are simple impressions, like "heroes" and "villains," "leaders" and "followers," the "lucky" and the "losers." I think these are templates that tell us what things mean. And I think they too come out of our biological nature.

Here's a short "story," about dogs, to suggest what I mean by stories.

"Hey, Mister, is that your dog? He seems to be enjoying himself, trotting ahead of you and then darting off into the hedge, then a few minutes later when you've walked on past him he comes racing after you and frisks at your side for a few moments before trotting on. What's he think he is, some kind of scout?

"He didn't look so friendly yesterday when I walked past your house. He came at me in a nasty stiff-legged walk and growled, his ears back and his teeth bared. He followed me down the road, barking and growling. A real hoodlum.

"Look at this, he's being friendly to me today, like we're pals. Well, he's no pal of mine. He and his real pals, two other dogs from your neighborhood, they killed a pig in my neighborhood last week on one of their hunting expeditions. They race through our yards like a gang looking for trouble . . ."

The dog has one set of stories when he's a watchdog in a territory-defending state, another when he's a scout for his master, and a third when he's hunting with his pack—then he's a hunter, or a colleague, or a challenger for the role of top dog, or killer, or any of perhaps a score of others. In each of these roles, he has a number of stories to tell, ready to succeed one another as situations change.

You may say animals don't tell themselves stories, as we do. But let me turn that around. Imagine a bird sitting on a branch. Suddenly it flies off to another tree, and perches there. What made it fly from one tree to another? Watch a cat. What makes it get up and walk off? Why does it want to come in for the twentieth time in a day?

There's something in animals that keeps them wandering, keeps them searching. I don't have a word for it. But whatever it is, in us I think it appears as stories.

6: *Turn meanings into words*

Now I'm ready to say where "meaning" in words comes from. The meanings of words are bits of the stories and the feelings we inherit, blended together.

Here's an example. The words "mother" and "father" have meanings for us coming from basic biology. Now take the two words, Mothercountry, and Fatherland. You can use these two words to describe the same plot of ground, but because of their associations with parent-words they have very different meanings. Mothercountry refers to the place where people live the way you were brought up. Fatherland refers to the place whose borders you're prepared to defend.

Extend that principle, combining sounds for bits of feelings and stories, and you can imagine all our words leading on one from another, blending together, all starting from the biological meanings of the stories and feelings the genome originally built into us. The result is all the words in a language, in which we can express our thoughts.

How about our values?
I think they're similar to meanings. But we use the two terms differently, and the difference seems to matter. So here's my definition: values are the meanings that matter most to us. The closer to our biological nature we get, the stronger those feelings and stories are going to be, and the more they rank as our values.

The origin of meaning isn't very mysterious. It's bits of our biology—gifts of the genome—that we humans have extended by making up words. But it's more than just adaptations to the environment. You need more than natural selection to account for it.

Meaning managers

Some people make it their business to develop a talent for identifying and managing meanings, perhaps expressing them through novels and scripts that can help us all learn how. From these we can all become more aware of the feelings and stories that motivate us.

There are directories that categorize novels by what human situations they deal with, so to become more sensitive to certain meanings you can simply order and read the appropriate novels!

Or go to the circus! You'll find some expert meaning managers there.

"How can I put meanings to work?"

Meanings as tools

Self help is basically about what things mean; they have one meaning now, you'd like them to mean something else later on, and you want a quick way to get from one to the other.

You could change the things themselves. Or instead of changing the things themselves you could just change the meanings they have for you.

Let's look at ways we can help our selves just by changing meanings.

"Reframing" your problems

"Reframing" something is changing what it means to you. It's very powerful. You "reframe" something by accounting for it in a different way. Know the phrase, "Sour grapes"? In a famous fable a wolf solved a problem of some grapes he wanted being out of his reach—he "reframed" his problem by telling himself the grapes were probably sour, anyway. Then his not being able to reach them didn't matter. By reframing the problem, he made it go away.

Start by identifying the key meanings involved in what's bothering you. Why are you angry? What are you afraid of? What's getting in the way? Now look for other meanings in the situation. Make it a story about the other person. Shift from the short-term to the long-term. Examples:

- Turn "I'm angry with my friend for telling lies about me" into "I'm glad she thought of using my name to get what she wanted, even if she did have to stretch the truth a bit."

- Turn "I'm angry at not getting that promotion" into "Maybe getting so angry is a sign I've been investing myself too much in my work. Maybe I should develop some interests outside work."

- Turn "I'm ashamed of not having the money to put my children through college" into "Education lasts so long these days, maybe you get a better start in life from real-world experience."

When you change those meanings, you may really solve your problem.

Being creative with meanings

Make up new meanings and you can reshape your world, and the worlds of other people, too.

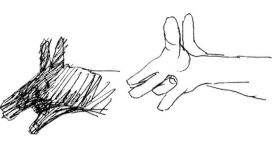

A friend of mine, Linda, invited a group of friends to her birthday party. They settled on an interesting form of celebration: they were each to bring a bead, a bead that expressed their relationship with Linda and their feelings towards her. At the celebration, they were each to say what their bead meant. The celebration ended with the beads being strung to make a necklace that was their joint birthday present.

The result was a necklace of truly incalculable value to those involved, because of all the meaning it carried. When Linda wears that necklace in that same group of friends, they will all know what each bead stands for. When Linda is with other people, she can describe her friends by going from bead to bead. Not only did they deliberately create meaning, they used an ingenious way of expressing and communicating it.

We are what things mean

Meanings aren't in the world outside. They're in us. The meanings in us will affect our experience of self-awareness.

I can measure my mood by just looking around me and noting how much meaning things seem to have. When I'm in a very good mood, I see rich meaning everywhere: in how things look, what associations they carry. I fall into reverie at the slightest thing: a steamed-up window, waving grass. The world becomes so pregnant with meaning that meaning starts to take precedence over matter, and I feel I'm in an enchanted world.

> *Thinking is meanings evolving in our minds. How well we can think will depend on the meanings we gathered and how well we manage them.*

CHAPTER 5

Gift 5:
Dreaming and consciousness

Something odd I've noticed about dreams—I remember myself experiencing them. I remember being aware of feelings, of thoughts, of enjoying meeting friends, of wondering about things, of being puzzled.

Here's an example: I dreamed I was sitting on a bench on a city street. Next to me on the bench were a mother and her son, perhaps 7 years old. She pointed to a skyscraper across the street that had a sculptured stone figure wrapped around a corner of the building about ten floors up. She mentioned a name, I took it to be the sculptor's name, and her son glanced over, and nodded.

I was impressed that a child so young could know something like that, and I wondered how she taught him the styles of sculptors. I was embarrassed that I didn't know the sculptor's name.

On waking, writing down dreams I notice I'm recalling my conscious experiences. I remember being conscious in the dream.

Which do you think came first, consciousness while dreaming, or consciousness while being awake? I think, consciousness while dreaming. That's what I think consciousness was originally created for. Maybe dreaming got created when mammals evolved, about 200 million years ago, long before we came along. We didn't invent dreaming.

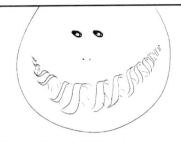

If there's an intelligent genome, why aren't we aware of it? Why can't we read its mind?

I think one answer is because, that's how we're made—we can't read minds. We can't read other people's minds, so why should we expect to read the mind of a genome?

How about the other way round? Can the genome read our mind?

I think it can. I think the genome can quiz us about our experiences. I think that's how it makes us report back.

How? First by making us conscious, then by making us dream.

I think the genome gave us consciousness as a way of communicating with us, in dreams, in terms of imaginary events and feelings.

What dreaming is for

When I dream, even though I'm the one doing the dreaming, I never know what's going to happen next.

It's as if I'm being tested—what will I do when this happens, when that happens? Is this frightening? Is that embarrassing? How do I feel? Dreams can seem like a quiz.

Dreams can also be lessons. Boys entering puberty have "wet dreams." I remember as a teenager being shaken awake in the middle of the night by lurid and extremely graphic visions of having sex. Living in a clergyman's home in London in the early 50's, those dreams were my first introduction to some of the behaviors that would be expected of me.

So dreams seem like two-way communication. They consist of situations I'm thrown into, to which I react. Either I'm being told what things mean. Or I'm reporting what they mean to me. I'm being taught, or I'm being quizzed.

Are our dreams different from our pets'? When our pets' paws twitch while they're sleeping, are they dreaming? I think so. Does this mean they're conscious when they're awake? I think so. When I wake up and remember what happened to me in my dreams, I "know" my waking conscious self is a continuation of my dreaming self. I don't see why that should be different in our pets.

Maybe any animal that dreams has consciousness, and can feel pain and suffering.

Where else but the genome could consciousness come from?

Can conscious experiences have an impact on the physical world, even though they're not physical themselves? Could they drive evolution?

I think they can. On waking we can recall conscious experiences we had while dreaming, so those experiences must have got stored in memory. That's something physical. If consciousness can do that it can drive our behavior. If we can drive our own behavior we can develop new habits. That can drive evolution. Maybe that's why the genome gave us consciousness.

CHAPTER 6

Gift 6:
Leftovers

Are our minds just bundles of disconnected adaptations, selected for one by one, which is what mutation and natural selection would be limited to creating?

That's not how the self feels to me. And that's not what a thinking genome is limited to creating. I'm going to assume the genome engineered for us a nicely rounded self that's more than the sum of a bunch of miscellaneous independent adaptations.

Sure, we can work against the genome's intention. We can easily splinter the self into a tree of twigs. We can separate body from mind, separate consciousness from the unconscious and split it further into left brain and right brain.

In this chapter let's put ourselves back together again. What we are, what we really are, is a body and a mind combined in a single human being. We're each a whole person.

Can we take advantage of being a whole person?

1. Personality

Why does it feel like something particular to be you? Where do you get your sense of who you are, what kind of person you are? What makes being you feel the way it does? What keeps that experience the same from one day to the next? I guess I'm asking, where does our personality come from?

The "thinking genome" story has an unusual answer. Each day, it suggests, our personality gets re-established for us in our dreams. We wake up already knowing who we are. Awake, we're the person we remember being in our dreams.

Is it the same person each day? Yes, as much as our body is the same body. As our body slowly ages, so does our personality. And as we can grow gray hair so we can lose or add pieces to that personality. They're both regulated by the same machinery inside us. What gets recreated each night for us in our dreams, is a restatement by the genome of who we are, told in terms of stories and feelings that we can understand, in our dreams. That tells us, each morning as we wake, decade by decade, who we are.

I do know I wake up already knowing who I am, from who I was in my dreams. My new self then quickly resets that "personality" to day-time logic and sensibleness.

That's first half-hour, though, is prime day-dreaming and creative time, when most of my best ideas emerge. I allow myself plenty of time to slumber after waking up. I may bring up something I need inspiration for, and see what happens.

2. Choose the right time frame

When you go looking for pleasure, watch out for "accommodation." That's not the place you sneak off to to enjoy yourself, it's a technical term for how desires fade on being satisfied. We "accommodate" to them.

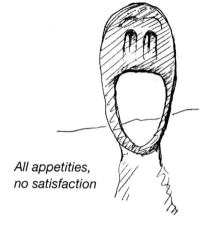

All appetites, no satisfaction

Desire, and this "accommodation," are engineering built into us to make us continuously seek whatever, in small doses, is good for us—food, sex, sleep. Once we've satisfied each desire, accommodation then dulls that desire's appeal, readying us for the appeal of the next. We're engineered to operate on a treadmill of a never-ending search for pleasure.

Until, that is, you get smart enough to say, "Stop the treadmill, I want to get off," and look for pleasures that don't accommodate so rapidly.

For wisdom about how long pleasures endure consider the Chinese proverb: "To be happy for a day get drunk, to be happy for a week get married, to be happy for a lifetime plant a garden."

Other pleasures beside gardening that can last a lifetime lie in "the humanities." The whole point of them used to be, making better selfs.

Think of a self as a tent all folded up. Studying the humanities can act to set up some posts, dig pins in all around, unfold the fabric, and stretch it over the posts by tightening the supporting ropes. Now the self has a capacious home to live in.

3. Taking Responsibility

Oops! I was hoping that word wouldn't come up. But there it is. I don't mean necessarily behaving responsibly, I mean taking responsibility for how you experience your self. Blaming your parents or your education really doesn't help much, because the only person who experiences your self is you. So only you are going to care enough to put things right.

Haunted by fears? Turn off the television. Distracted? Turn off the music.

Part of taking responsibility is going to be figuring things out. Think you're not smart enough? Don't worry. The genome's built wonderful capabilities into you. Look within, and explore.

4. The park bench

Every so often, take your new self for a spin. Go sit on a park bench for half an hour. What's it feel like being you? Realize there's something you're missing? Visit the video store or library and bone up on it. Reconnect with an old friend who might help. Join a group. Then take yourself for a spin on that park bench again. Repeat as necessary until you feel satisfied with your self.

Summary of Handbook 1

Concious selfs are sources of enormous complexity and power. The whole world has been transformed by them. Look around, every bridge, every road, originated in a self. Almost everything on Earth except deserts, rivers and clouds has been transformed by selfs. You can't begin to account for today's world without paying tribute to the enormous impact on it of selfs. It's conscious selfs that have so transformed the matter of the earth, not just bodies made of matter.

And each of us has a self.

How can we make the most of our conscious self? I don't think science can't help us. Science works best with whatever repeats with material precision. Evolution is precisely the opposite, it's the source of all ingenuity and novelty. To enrich the self we need ideas drawn not from science but from the study of evolution. In this first handbook I look for the origin of each aspect of the self in evolution's massive creative power, then suggest how to draw some of that creative power down into the self.

Self and science—which is larger?
Science arose inside people's consciousness, so the conscious self is larger.

The scientific and evolutionary points of view highlight different aspects of the self.

- Science highlights aspects of the self it can give a material account for, such as the senses.

- Evolution highlights those that give living creatures most opportunity to direct their own evolution, such as consciousness.

If what you're interested in is how to solve problems involving the self, I suggest you take your lead from evolution.

2
Handbook

Harnessing the processes

What makes our species unique? And how did our ancestors use that to create civilization and our modern self? Building on the logic of the intelligent-genome theory I come up with some suggestions.

Then we made ourselves even more special. We created language. And we discovered evolution. Can we put those two achievements together, and come up with a new way for talking about our selfs and how they evolved?

I suggest how. In place of the words "mutation," "natural selection" and "adaptation." I propose "intelligent trial and error," "transactions," and "engines of evolution." I suggest how we can shape our thinking around these evolutionary processes.

Then, how to deal with the combination of the original self and our new civilized self.

Finally, creativity. I propose abandoning words like "free" and "determined" drawn from physics and replacing them with terms based on evolution. We're as free and creative as evolution itself, no more, no less.

CHAPTER 1

Technology so advanced it's magic

Beep! Beep! The spaceship from Alpha Centauri settles on the ground, a hatch opens and two aliens emerge. "Take us to your leader," says one.

But you're not interested in anything these little green men have to say. You brush past them and enter the space ship. How does this thing work? What technologies does it have built into it that we could apply here on Earth?

How advanced is the technology of life? Recall what happens when an animal dies.

Immediately, waves of chemical breakdown race through its body, its tissues start to digest themselves, it very quickly putrifies.

This means that, every second that creature was alive, this putrefaction was being held at bay. Someone or something was smart enough to keep that from happening every second, for maybe decades, even a century.

This isn't merely something difficult, it's something absolutely stupendously miraculous, way beyond any other kind of machinery we know about.

Actually we don't need the spaceship from Alpha Centauri. We're planetary rovers ourselves. Strangely, unlike the planetary rovers NASA sends to other planets, we're soft. We seem like something made out of putty rather than a sophisticated piece of engineering. But that's what we are.

Can you imagine what kind of mathematics, measuring instruments, chemical equipment, you'd need to create and maintain something like us? No you can't, nor can I, nor can anyone. Most of it is still way beyond our imagining. To us it's advanced enough to seem like magic.

Wouldn't it be great to get our hands on all that technology! Behind the dashboard and the controls that the genome put within easy reach, there's all the technology you need to build such a rover and keep it running.

Well, we did get our hands on some of that technology. The genome gave us—and only us—tools to tap into some of it. Our ancestors used those tools to create, first, civilization, then a new self.

In this chapter I take the measure of some of those technologies.

A magic blueprint

When I stretch my two arms out in front of me and bring the palms of my hands together, my two arms are almost exactly the same length.

No!

Why is that so surprising? Whatever codes in me for arm-length doesn't come with a fixed length written into it. So how does it get my arm lengths just right, in proportion to my height?

And how does it keep them both the same length? From the time my two arms budded off from my embryo a few weeks after conception, those two arms have been growing on opposite sides of my body out of sight of each other, until now when I stretch my arms out sideways my two hands are nearly six feet apart. So how, at any one moment, does one arm know how long the other one's got? And assuming it begins growing faster to catch up, how would it know when to stop?

Now take my two hands. Remember, my two hands have grown up separated from each other by nearly six feet of arm and chest.

Any signal from one has to pass through six feet of body tissue to reach the other. Yet when I bring my two hands together with the palms facing me, I see they're almost identical. If you don't think that's surprising, put your right hand up against someone else's left hand and see how different the hands of different people can be.

Strange! My two hands are almost exactly the same, except in one fundamental way. They're mirror images of each other.

How does the genome do that ? Of course, it could code separately for a left-hand version and a right-hand version, but then it's unlikely our two hands would be so precisely alike, any more alike than our left hand is like our left foot.

No, it seems more likely that both hands are made from the same blueprint. My body can use these blueprints to make arms, hands, whatever it needs. And it keeps referring to these blueprints to keep my arms growing at the same rate, until they reach the appropriate length.

How do you fit a blueprint into a molecule?

Repair and maintenance

"Fix it!"

A newt can regrow almost any part of its body, including the brain, spinal cord, heart, and limbs. The Zebra fish can regenerate its heart. And I've read that, up to the age of nine, a child can regrow the entire top joint of a finger.

How is that possible? How does a stump of ripped flesh and shattered bone know how to regrow all the missing bits, getting them all in the right place, and know when to stop growing so it ends up the right length? That isn't how the missing piece originally grew; it grew as part of an embryo, everything growing up together all at once, a totally different process.

In fact, repair is going on all the time.
The human body tosses out and replaces all its matter every three months or so. Iron in your blood, calcium in your bones, everything. That means that after several months there's nothing left of the old you. Yet here you still appear to be, the same person, thinking much the same thoughts.

To me this seems quite miraculous. If you or I were to replace all the stuff something is made of with new stuff, no matter how carefully we did it, it wouldn't go back exactly the same way, in exactly the same place. It would gradually develop bends and crooks as the new materials went back just slightly differently from how the old materials went. That's just how the world is.

Yet in the body, everything stays just the way it was. Can you imagine how something like that would revolutionize how we make things if we were smart enough to figure it out?

What mechanical mastery must that take, that the genome has at its disposal!

Sins forgiven

How come, when I drink half a bottle of wine with dinner, I suffer nothing worse than a mild and short-lived intoxication?

My body is an enormously, enormously complex assemblage of machinery. It's far more complex than a real planetary rover. Everything takes place in a liquid environment of slightly salty water that bathes every part and carries supplies to and fro just so.

Yet I can pour an ounce and a half of ethyl alcohol, a very different solvent, into it, and almost nothing happens. In fact, I can pour quite a variety of solvents into my body and, apart from a temporary hiccup, my body will guide itself firmly back to its equilibrium condition. I can even lose pints of water from my body, as people do when they get lost in a desert, or flood my system with gallons of beer, and my system will take it all in its stride and bring itself back to the state it obviously considers normal.

Add chemistry to the technologies the genome is a master of.

CHAPTER 2

Forging civilization and a new self

First of the tools the genome gave to us, and us alone, was a master wrench for taking off the rover's control panel and plugging directly into those advanced technologies.

Every so often, someone uses that master wrench to tap into those technologies. We call these people prodigies, people who display powers way beyond what seems possible for people of their age or training.

Prodigies

Here's an 8-year old from the 19th century:

"**On being asked** the SQUARE ROOT of 106,929, he answered 327 before the original number could be written down. He was then required to find the cube root of 268,336,125, and with equal facility and promptness he replied 645.

"He was asked how many minutes there are in 48 years, and before the question could be taken down he replied 25,228,800, and immediately afterwards he gave the correct number of seconds.

"On being requested to give the factors which would produce the number 247,483, he immediately named 941 and 263, which are the only two numbers from the multiplication of which it would result.

"On being interrogated as to the manner in which he obtained these results, the boy constantly said he did not know HOW the answers came into his mind... in the extraction of roots, and in the discovery of the factors of large numbers, it did not appear that any operation COULD take place, since he gave answers IMMEDIATELY, or in a very few seconds, which, according to the ordinary methods, would have required very difficult and laborious calculations, and prime numbers cannot be recognized as such by any known rule."

Similar feats, in languages, games such as chess, and music composition, have been found in children as young as three.

Now for the second marvelous tool the genome gave us.

What is it that most separates us from all other living creatures, even our nearest relatives, the apes? According to my story so far, it's not consciousness; animals had been conscious for many millions of years before we came along. Is it walking upright? Is it our hands, and being able to make and use tools? Is it speech? Is it intelligence? Is it our larger brain? Is it...

When you have so many candidates for what makes us special, that's a clue it isn't any one of those, it's something else that lies behind them all. What tool could the genome have built into us, that all these others build on?

I'm going to say it's a talent for mimicry.

Mimicry is common in living creatures. Insects evolve to look like leaves or twigs, the chameleon and the octopus evolved to change color to match their surroundings, harmless butterflies evolve to resemble poisonous ones, parrots can imitate almost any sound they hear.

But the mimicry champions of the world are we humans. We can make up ways to mimic things, on the fly. And that's what I think is basic to being a human being. I see all our distinctive attributes coming from our ability to make up new ways of mimicking each other and other creatures, and the world around us, as the need arises.

"What am I?"

Here's a game that was popular a century or more ago—charades. One person silently mimes something, the other players have to guess what it is. As they blurt out suggestions, the performer mimes further clues to help them, until someone comes up with the answer. That person then becomes the performer.

Now imagine something like this around 3 million years ago. You could think of charades as our first communications revolution.

Speech, chanting and worksongs

Put together mimicry, and prodigies able to tap into the genome's more advanced technologies, and what do you get? Eventually, civilization.

Speech probably came from us mimicking animal cries, and our own cries! Speech probably led to chanting. And chanting, I'm going to suppose, led to the first technological breakthrough"

Difficulties overcome by the original inventors of speech

Worksongs

Imagine you've tying a knot. As you go you make up a song about it. To make the same knot later, making the right movements in the right order, you recall and recite the same song. We have remnants of something like that in our "Here's the church and here's the steeple, open the church and there's the people" and playing cats cradle. We tick things off on our hands. Boys use their fists while reciting chants like "paper, stone, scissors" or "one potato, two potato..." to pick teams.

An early computer

All the wisdom needed for quite complicated behaviors could be stored in worksongs. Eventually, a whole community could be driven by collections of worksongs, from top to bottom, to make bricks or build a wall. Or, really, whatever you wanted.

Remember those occasional prodigies who seem to break into the rover's toolbox and access some of its behind-the-scenes technologies? By their achievements being mimicked in the form of work songs their skills could be recorded and transmitted to other people.

Those skills could get passed down from one generation to another in families, each family specializing in a single skill—counting, measuring, surveying, starting fires, pottery glazing, ritual, etc. Several families pooling their worksong-skills could form an industry.

Communities with industries like that could get together to form a city. And huge cities did appear, with thousands of people practicing skills no other animal ever had.

Writing and reason

Then someone invented the alphabet, and all the skills needed for running a huge city, such as counting, arithmetic, writing and reading, singing, drawing, fighting, building furnaces, managing livestock, riding horses, growing and harvesting wheat, brewing, politicking, public speaking, and so on, all those skills could be written down and taught to children in school.
When these children grew up they would combine all these mental skills in a single body of wisdom.

A new self had been created.

A third tool:
we can drive our own evolution

Here's another marvellous tool the genome built into us—our inventions can become built into our genes. Learning languages is in our genes, we start learning how as infants. At least two parts of our brains are devoted to speech and language. They must have been used for something else originally, but once we invented speech they evolved to support language.

So it looks as if culture can turn into genes in just a few tens of thousands of years. That's another way we're special, unique among living creatures. Who knows what else in our nature, in our genes, got there because of people imitating things, trying out new ideas?

This is another example of thinking becoming evolving, only in this case it's individual people doing the thinking, not the genome.

Alfred Wallace

This book is dedicated to the 19th century naturalist and collector Alfred Wallace. He beat Charles Darwin in submitting the idea of natural selection for publication, so he's regarded as one of its two discoverers.

But a few years later he changed his mind. Natural selection could not be the only mechanism of evolution, he announced, because it could not account for how we acquired the talents needed to create civilization. That meant there must be some other processes that drove human evolution.

And if that was true, maybe those processes, and not natural selection, were responsible for all of evolution.

Process 1:
Intelligent trial and error

Can we incorporate more of the genome's wisdom into the new self we got from becoming civilized?

In this and the next two chapters I point to processes I think an intelligent genome would employ to evolve better creatures, and I suggest ways we could apply those processes to enhance our selfs.

Trial and error—you know what that is. You come up with an idea you think might work, you try it, if it works you apply it. And if you're a human being, or the genome itself, you apply this process using your intelligence. That's intelligent trial and error.

In the case of the genome, the ideas in question are actual living creatures. The genome uses them as probes into the world they live in. They're like questions the genome poses to the world. The answers it gets it can apply to dreaming up new and even better probes.

Let's suppose the genome's imagined some ingenious new equipment it would like to try out. It would think the necessary new genes into a few individuals, and through their dreams, say, follow their success or failure. Failure would tell it to not implement the idea. Success would tell it to apply that change more widely.

Can we apply intelligent trial and error in our thinking, the way I'm supposing the genome does?

Don't make any more of these

Not only can we, we already do. Business uses intelligent trial and error to come up with new ideas and refine them. Once we understand these processes, we can apply them in our own thinking and turn them into powerful tools for self help.

How intelligent trial and error works

Think of intelligent trial and error as a cycle:
- intelligent variation
- followed by intelligent selection
- followed by more variations.

You base your new variations on the variation that was most successful the last time.

As you repeat the cycle, your variations will keep getting better.

There are three things you can vary:

* How you come up with the variations,

* how you test them (selection)

* how many times you repeat the cycle.

Three examples of how business exploits all three parts of the cycle.

Brainstorming

* Helps you come up with new ideas.

* Focus is on variation.

* Lasts only one cycle.

First, get a group of creative people together. Encourage them to be creative—give them colored pencils and large pads of paper to doodle on.

Tell them the problem, and ask them to come up with the wildest solutions they can think of. Help them by asking ridiculous questions like, "What would a cat do" (or a dog, or an elephant), "Imagine this problem was on Mars," "What would Napoleon have done?"

None of this

Don't let people criticize or judge each other's ideas. Instead, encourage them to bounce ideas off each other as quickly as possible, to come up with as many wild and creative suggestions as possible.

Once they've run out of ideas, let them all go. The brainstorming part is over. On your own you can switch to selection. First, you decide which ideas have promise, then you look for ways to actually apply them. Or you can use those ideas as raw material for the other two processes.

Here's an example of business using brainstorming. An electric power company was looking for ways to keep its power lines from breaking under the weight of winter snow. During a brainstorming session, someone suggested having birds flap their wings over the electric lines to shake the snow off. That idea got translated into having helicopters fly over the power lines from end to end during snowstorms to blow the snow loose.

Focus groups

- Help you select the best alternative.

- Focus is on selection.

- Can last one or several cycles.

Example: a publisher wants to test a new kind of magazine.

The editor brings a dozen people together around a table in a special meeting room. They're strangers to one another, all chosen because they read similar kinds of magazines.

They're shown three versions of a new magazine. These have been made to look just like real magazines you'd buy in a store. The participants examine these copies of the magazine, answer question from a moderator, and vote for which version they like best.

Often, one wall of the room will be a half-silvered mirror. The publisher and her marketing and editorial staff sit quietly behind the mirror, invisible to the participants, watching and listening to the participants' reactions to the different versions of the magazine. Those reactions help the editor settle on the final form of the magazine.

The Delphi method

- Helps you refine an idea.

- Uses both variation and selection.

- Goes through several cycles.

Suppose you want help coming up with the best possible decision. You find several people whose advice you trust, and you ask them for their opinions. Those are your initial variations.

Then you repeat this process several more times, but now, each time, you copy all the opinions you received and feed back them back to everyone. In the light of everyone else's opinion each one gives you a new opinion.

Gradually, as you repeat this cycle, one idea is likely to emerge, more powerful and subtle than any of the ideas people came up with originally.

That final idea is the sum of all your experts' wisdom.

More powerful than any one alone

> *"For me, evolution involving intelligent trial and error isn't just theory. I detect the process taking place, at lightning speed, in my own thinking, when I make puns."*

Punning

Punning involves two cycles of trial and error. First, a punster continuously scans the words in other people's remarks, looking for variations of them that have some humor potential. If one of those variations shows some promise, the punster then looks for various replies employing that variation.

If one of these replies "works," then, after two cycles, the punster delivers this reply aloud, ideally without any pause in the conversation. It's a very, very rapid process of trial and error—variations on the other person's words, variations on remarks including that word, then delivery of the selected remark.

She loved it when I made puns

Here's an example that illustrates this double-cycle process.

My wife said to me, "I hear Ireland's booming." "Oh," I said, "You can hear it from here?" ("Here" being America's Hudson Valley, 3000 miles away.)

Notice the two steps I had to go through. I first had to notice that she had unconsciously made a pun, that "I hear" and "booming" both had alternative meanings related to sound.

Then I had to scout for various formulations of a response that referred to those "sound" meanings instead of the meaning she'd intended, selecting the one that made the most sense as a reply.

I can observe this process going on in the background while I'm listening to someone. Sometimes the hunt for variations on the meanings of the words they use just peters out, with no good pun being found, and that's when I'm particularly aware of the process, in the pointlessness of all the variations.

Why do I do it? I've concluded punning is just a by-product of thinking itself, a sort of waste product, like chips piling up when you whittle wood. It's just a byproduct of the intelligent trial and error process that underlies all of evolution, including our own thinking.

"No, but seriously, how can I put this to use?"

You can apply these techniques to your own thinking. In fact, it's likely you already do, unconsciously.

Here, in essence, is how the cycle of intelligent trial and error repeats:

- You select your best idea, and think up variations of it.

- You select the best of these ideas, and think up variations of it.

- You select the best of these ideas, and think up variations of it.

And so on.

To refine the process you could brainstorm alone, feed the ideas you like best into a Delphi-like process with a few friends by email to decide which work best, then try out the final result by getting a few more friends together in a focus group.

You can string these steps in any order. Do it consciously and deliberately at first and it should eventually become an extension of your regular thinking.

Darwinists would like you to believe the combination of mutation and natural selection works through this kind of process.

But it doesn't. It doesn't come up with intelligently created variations, only random variations most of which are bound to be harmful.

And it can't test them intelligently before building them into the genome, it's not efficient enough.

So in each generation the combination of mutation and natural selection would let through into the genome many more damaging mutations than promising ones.

In a few generations, end of species!

"Natural selection and intelligent trial and error aren't real. You won't trip over them. They don't exist the way actual living creatures do. They're just ideas someone made up.

"The point of them is to help us make sense of things. That's how I settled on what I'm calling the three 'processes' behind evolution, like intelligent trial and error and, coming up, transactions. If I'm successful they'll help us make sense of our selves and trace connections between our selves and the rest of evolution.

"But they're just ideas. There could really be five processes, or fifty. And if you don't like mine, make up your own. That's what Charles Darwin and Alfred Wallace did."

CHAPTER 4

Process 2:
Transactions

If there's anything like an atom in evolution, for me that would be an individual transaction.

According to this "atomic" theory, evolution is the product of trillions and trillions of transactions:

- transactions between each creature and each element in its world,

- transactions between insects and the flowers they pollinate,

- transactions between us and our garden plants and our pets,

- transactions between us and our friends,

- transactions between one idea and another.

That, I'm suggesting, is the process behind the works of the greatest artists, the theories of the most brilliant scientists, the apparent perfection of animals and plants. If you give enormous numbers of "transactions" enough time they'll lead to extreme creativity.

We already know this. We know that our massed financial transactions create an economy, and our massed buyings and sellings create a marketplace. These entities once didn't exist, but now they do, because of our massed transactions.

In fact, when we see massed transactions, we take it for granted they'll cause complex changes. If we see a new kind of massed transaction, such as Facebook or Twitter, we know it will bring about some kind of evolution, even though we can't predict what the results will be.

To qualify as a transaction, an occasion must be unpredictable; if the occasion is predictable, nothing new can develop. And there must be something at stake.

Because of this, a transaction will involve risk, but it will also offer opportunity.

In a way, it's like gambling. But while in gambling the odds are stacked against you, in transactions the odds would be stacked in your favor.

Each individual transaction may be unpredictable. But massed transactions, by harnessing the small possibilities for creativity within each individual transaction, could become so powerful they'd be irresistible.

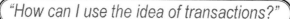

"How can I use the idea of transactions?"

If evolution does involve transactions where something significant is at risk, then you should be able to change your self by subjecting it to some new transactions. An example for me was learning how to draw. I really had no choice, I could learn to draw only through continual practice, but I was able to speed up progress by making sure each effort involved both something to be gained plus risk of failing.

However you want to help your self it's probably a good idea to embark on a succession of small transactions than to submit your self or someone else to a single live-or-die transaction.

Suppose you're trying to move grandma into a retirement home. That's a big change. Attempt to achieve it in one step and she's likely to dig in her heels and refuse. But break the transition down into a series of smaller transactions and you can make the process easier, maybe turning up benefits along the way that can make the move actually welcome. Invite some residents in the retirement home round for tea, for example.

Process 3:
Engines of evolution

What's makes evolution so creative? Is it the sheer number of living creatures and how quickly they reproduce?

That's what you'd think if it was natural selection what drove evolution. Huge numbers of tiny creatures reproducing every few hours would give natural selection maximum chances to take effect.

But over time, as creatures got bigger, their populations got smaller and generations came further apart, with fewer young per generation to select from.

Each of these changes would give natural selection fewer opportunities to do its work and you'd expect evolution to slow down.

But that's not what happened. Instead evolution seems to be going as fast as ever, if not faster.

Examples of evolution's speed

Take the evolution of whales from a land animal something like a horse. That involved a huge number of major changes: turning its front legs into flippers, losing its back legs, reshaping its tail and its skull (nostrils moving to the top of its head), having to cope with the salt in sea water, and adjusting to a new diet. That's like turning a combine harvester into a submarine.

Imagine the age of the Earth compressed down to one hour. All that evolution would have happened in about a second, just a few seconds ago. The evolution of humans from a chimpanzee-like ancestor would have taken less than the hour's final half a second. Despite natural selection having fewer opportunities to take effect, evolution's racing.

"Let's go scuba!"

Clearly evolution can't be driven by natural selection. So what does drive it?

You know what I think—evolution's driven by the thinking of the intelligent genome. But what makes it go so rapidly?

I've another idea: engines of evolution. As the genome matured it evolved "engines" to make evolution work faster and faster.

You've probably already come across what I'm calling "engines of evolution" in school biology class.

Cooperation, for example.

- The cells of our own bodies are built out of a community of originally-independent organisms that opted to set up home together.,

- The tiny "plant," Lichen, is an intimate mixture of two very different creatures, algae and fungus.

- Mammals depend on a multitude of bacteria to help them digest food.

- Human evolution has been helped along by collaboration between humans and horses, and humans and dogs.

Another "engine of evolution" that's recently been discovered is genes that control development. With these the genome could grow larger and more complex creatures—first yeast cells, then fish, mammals, and humans.

Other engines of evolution are nerve cells getting gathered together into brains, and social life in insects and mammals.

"Once you think of evolution this way, isn't it obvious evolution's been driven by a succession of engines like this, from the beginning?

"That's the real story of evolution, not the creation of species but how the genome came up with new engines of evolution. And this idea of engines driving evolution faster and faster provides us with a great opportunity to use the powers of evolution to enhance our selfs."

Engines of evolution would be what give transactions much of their power. Transactions would usually involve intelligent trial and error, applied to one or another engine of evolution.

For self help, we'll usually use engines of the evolution of culture. They've driven evolution faster and faster.

- From fire to farming took a million or so years.

- From the printing press to the computer took just a few hundred.

- From the computer to the Internet took just a few decades.

There are engines of cultural evolution all around us. Here are some more examples:

- Making fire. Tools. Clothing. Money. Paper.

- Counting. Measuring. Reciting. Writing. Acting. Ritual. Drawing. Music.

- Pageantry. Politics. Democracy. Theater. Education.

- Stock markets. Mass production. Telecommunications.

- Double entry bookkeeping. The idea of atoms. Novels.

- Steam and gasoline engines. Cameras. Computer programming.

Got a problem you can divide into separate transactions? To drive each transaction faster and more surely review the list and select an appropriate engine.

- Money: reward your self for each success.

- Use paper notes to monitor some process

- Establish a ritual to help you through some process

- Memorize a series of steps by checking them off on your fingers?

- Use metal, fire, air, water, a balloon, a paperweight, a car, a flashlight, to help you solve a problem.

Adapting the processes of evolution to thinking

Thinking about the self in terms of "natural selection," "genetic mutation" and "adaptation" is bound to limit what we expect of it. Can we think in terms that will lead us to expect more? I've come up with "intelligent trial and error," "transactions," and "engines of evolution."

I based those terms on the assumption there's intelligence in the processes of evolution. But most scientists would disagree. They grant that individual living creatures—all products of evolution—can be intelligent. But they insist that that other product of evolution, the genome, isn't. By denying intelligence to the process of evolution they set limits to what we can expect of the self.

I think they're wrong. I see intelligence as key to all three of the processes of evolution I identified in this handbook.

- Variation is the result of intelligent trial and error, eliminating the need for much of the selection required in Darwinism.

- Evolution happens through transactions that are intelligently identified and undertaken.

- Over time evolution intelligently devises ever-better engines for driving evolution.

In the last three chapters I suggested how we can draw on these evolutionary processes to enhance how we think. But if thinking is evolving, we should be able to apply to evolution terms we use to describe our own thinking.

- "Mind" is a hypothetical place where we can imagine evolution happening—it's hard to think about thinking and evolving without imagining them happening somewhere.

- "Thinking" is thoughts evolving, in this "mind."

- "Evolution" is the genome, or us, thinking creatively.

- Consciousness is experiencing evolution taking place, in "mind."

CHAPTER 6

Our two selfs become one self aware

Have you ever said to yourself, "Whatever made me do that! I should have my head examined!"

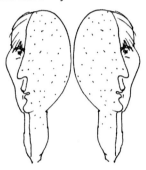

Well, you just did. One part of your head examined and passed judgment on another part. New Year's resolutions—we make them, then we break them. One part of us wants to change, but another part of us says "no." Fairly often we do seem to be in two minds.

Once the genome gave us tools to access some of its more powerful technologies, the human brain saturated itself with speech, worksongs, and alphabetic writing.

The result was a new, civilized, self.

But as a result, people found their consciousness home to two waking selfs: the original "natural" self the Earth rover came with, and this new self that came along with civilization. Over time these two selfs have had to learn to get along.

We house the same two selfs today, and have the same problem of learning how to manage them.

The old self comes with its original guarantee, straight from the genome. But the new self is like an aftermarket add-on. You can't return it for repairs. It's not part of our original specs.

So managing this new self, and its relations to the old self, is up to us.

How can we get our two selfs to work together?

Telling the two selfs apart

Our original self

The self we come by naturally is the kind of self our pets have, smart, impulsive, emotional. It's the part of us that acts pretty automatically, greets people naturally, laughs easily, gets upset, and so on.

This is the default self, always idling in the background. It's the self that's conscious in dreams, that communicates during dreaming with the genome.

The two selfs store their wisdom in different ways.

- The new self uses mainly words and mathematics and musical notations, things you can write down.

- The original self uses a language of its own that the new self often can't read.

This is like a computer word-processor not being able to read a file made by a graphics program like Photoshop. Even though they're saved on the same hard disk, they store information differently, so they can't read one another's files.

Since our two selfs can't read each other's "minds," they have to dialog together, in our heads, like an odd couple. I think we find comedy duos amusing because they mirror in public what most of the time is actually happening in our heads.

The original self can use language, but it's limited. In one dream I was amused by a sort of pun, but when I woke up it made no sense. My dreaming self didn't seem to know how to handle puns.

Our new self

This self embeds itself in us in infancy and childhood as we learn and use language. Language takes over and organizes part of our brain, and becomes part of us. By the time we're old enough to decide whether we want this second self or not, it's too late. We're stuck with it.

During sleep it's shut down, and it may get turned off at other times too.

Other differences

Comedy duo?

The original self can learn habits. That's important because most of self improvement consists of learning new habits. The original self can run us out of habit while we're "consciously" doing something else. It can run several habits at once, such as whistling "absent-mindedly" as it drives, while the new self concentrates on what we're going to say when we arrive.

The new self has no problem letting the original self manage things through habits. Some of those habits the new self teaches the original self, through driving lessons, for example. Our two selfs must work together closely like this all the time.

But both selfs are plugged directly into the same consciousness. As a result each self is aware of the other, and becomes aware of itself. This is where I see self-consciousness coming from.

Language is ten thousand years of civilization boiled down for rapid learning and easy storage

"How can I get my two selfs to help themselves?"

Knowing about the two selfs can help you work out what's going to be involved in self-help. Suppose you want to become a trapeze artist. Expect your new self to have to teach your original self some very elaborate new habits, over and over again, involving a lot of humiliating failure. Can both your selfs take all that failure? Will the eventual payoff in sensual pleasure be enough reward for the original self? Or is your goal the income you'll earn as a professional, more of a new-self reward?

Traditional ways we think about the self won't help us here. Christianity's God gave you a "you," a single self, so you could tell right and wrong, and as long as you chose to do right He took responsibility for the consequences.

But if you take over from God and manage your own self then you become responsible for what happens, and whether you're better off.

The phantasy version of self help is three magic wishes. A genie grants you three wishes that will bring about whatever you wish.

The usual comeuppance in stories about three wishes, of course, is that people end up worse than they started. They ask for the wrong things. Either they don't know what it is they really want, or they forget what comes along with what they ask for.

Creativity

"I've been a graphic designer, a book designer, science writer, webmaster and entrepreneur. I draw, paint, exhibit photos, and write novels. I'm an inventor with a patent.

"So why am I writing a book on evolution?

"I'm doing it to defend the conscious self and creativity. People hire me to be creative. It's my stock-in-trade. All my hobbies are creative. Creativity is vital to me. So when creativity comes under attack I rush to its defense.

"And creativity is under attack. It's under attack from science."

According to science, creativity can't exist because it would contradict physics.

Physics says everything at a human scale is predictable so there's no room in physics for the self to be free to be creative. Or for creativity in evolution.

To account for evolution—including the evolution of a creative self—science came up with a purely physical explanation: mutation and natural selection. That's molecules getting corrupted, then sorted according to which ones end up in creatures that survive. That's what children are being taught in the school science classroom. They're told they're made by a process that's purely physical, that can make only physical things.

Obviously, if that's true then we can't have evolved to become conscious. A purely physical process couldn't do that. They may not actually be told that, but that's an obvious implication.

The people who teach this, what do they think consciousness is?

To them it's like the viewfinder on a camera. The viewfinder can tell you what the camera's pointed at but it can't take the picture. Consciousness is just a monitor that can tell you what's going on in your brain, it can't change anything there.

What drives your behavior is not your conscious decisions, it's brain chemistry.

You're a robot.

I've been there. For years I believed only physical things could make anything happen in the physical world. Everything I did was determined not by my consciousness but by chemical reactions in my body and my brain.

What's that feel like? Great. I felt very sophisticated. I was proud of myself for believing something that other people thought contradicted common sense. I knew what was really going on, they were living under a delusion.

Then one day I had an amazing revelation! I realized I was wrong. I realized there was no dark corner of consciousness concealed from matter that I couldn't speak or write about. And speaking and writing are clearly things happening in the real, physical world. I'd been expressing my conscious thoughts through physical actions all along, just like everyone else.

This hit me like a thunderbolt. I suddenly became aware of something absolutely extraordinary that most people didn't give a moment's thought to—the physical world can interact with consciousness, and consciousness can interact with the physical world. They're doing it all the time, all around us. It's in our buildings, it's in the litter lying by the side of the road, it's in every gesture and sound we make. This is absolutely certain.

Yet science refuses to recognize it, to say anything about it.

Ever since then I've felt the passion of a convert. I've felt it's my duty to warn people if I see them in danger of becoming a robot.

Here's what I tell them.

"Stop thinking about your self in terms of physics, whether it's free or determined. Instead, think of your self in terms of the creativity in evolution. What did it take for the genome to cover the Earth with hundreds of millions of species of living creatures over billions of years? Whatever that was, obviously it didn't conflict with physics.

"The genome built that same freedom and creativity into your self. Don't dismiss it."

How can we become more creative?

We can become more creative by using the processes of evolution in our own thinking. For me, that's through sequences of transactions involving intelligent trial and error and engines of evolution.

Interior decorators, fashion designers; they all employ intelligent trial and error. First you rapidly sketch some basic designs. Then you pick one and make as many variations of it as you can. Then you pick the best one of those and use it as a basis of further variations, over and over. As you go the concepts keep getting better. In a graphic designer's sketchpad you can often pick out this process, recorded in sequences of sketches, each one exploring possibilities in the best sketches of the sequence before.

Samples of advertising design from my portfolio

Fashion designers and architects may play with other engines of evolution besides sketching. Fire, for example—a fashion designer might experiment by scorching various fabric. The famous architect Frank Gerhy plays around with paper shapes in designing his building. Painters may wear colored spectacles to explore their subject matter, or distort photos of it on the computer. And of course artists are always looking for ideas from the past they could use.

Professional creatives instinctively work the way I described, going through series of transactions using intelligent trial and error and drawing on engines of evolution. But everyone can learn how, by deliberately setting out to follow that process until it becomes a habit.

Follow the master

3

Finding new meaning

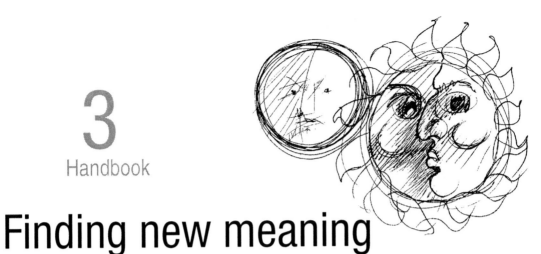

*Where can we find the wisdom we crave?
In this handbook we look at meanings we can
get from biology in general, from Darwinism, and from the theory of the intelligent
genome.*

*Beyond meaning, can we find in the theory
of the intelligent genome a new mission?
A couple of hints are explored.*

*Following this handbook you'll find "Tips on
adopting a new self." Having a choice of selfs
was common and understood in the past.
But with the rise of Christianity we got used
to the idea that there could be only one right
kind of self, and our job was to make everyone adopt it.*

*Can we once again enjoy a choice of selfs? A
choice between Darwinisn and Lamarckism,
for example?*

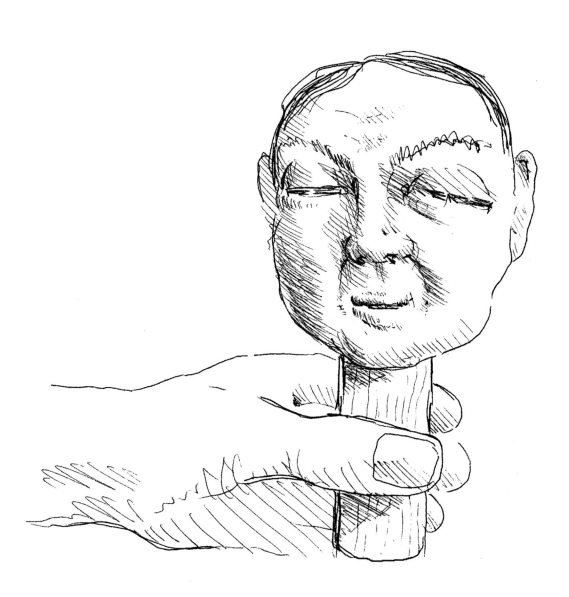

CHAPTER 1

Managing meaning

What's the meaning of life?

The answer's easy—for every creature but us. The meaning of other creatures' lives is whatever meanings the genome programmed into them. Only humans have a problem coming up with an answer. The meanings the genome programmed into our old self don't satisfy our new self, or our new self-aware joint self. We demand more meaning.

To make the problem worse, we live in the shadow of a super-intense body of meaning. Notice the super-rich chunks of meaning in these two short sentences:

> *"God loves us and has given us the price-*
> *less gift of an immortal soul. If we repay*
> *those gifts by choosing to worship and*
> *love Him, we'll go to Heaven and live in*
> *Paradise with Him forever."*

In Christian countries until just a few centuries ago this was the ultimate meaning shared by almost everyone. I think it still sets the standard for how much meaning we expect out of life. But are we getting it?

Could consciousness itself be the meaning in life? We could simply try to make our selfs as conscious as possible.

But we might end up worse off than we were before. I could find I'm more easily bored when my new bigger consciousness isn't fully occupied. And my experience of grief and other tormenting conscious states might become unendurable. Developing consciousness itself may not automatically be a good idea.

Currently we're coasting along making do with meanings in the words we inherit. We inherit one set of words from the Greeks, another set from Christianity. From the Greeks we get words such as quantity, quality, logic, psychology and criticism. From Christianity we get pity, gentle, mercy, anguish, beauty, bounty, charity, comfort, courtesy, delicate, devotion, grace, honor, humble, patient, peace, purity, tender, pathos, pathetic, long-suffering, conscience, passion and compassion.

Useful words, but they're mostly byproducts of old meaning systems. They wear out. Worn-out words include honor, duty, chastity and obligation.

As our vocabulary wears out, our need for new meaning becomes more pressing

Can we get back, instead of forward, back to some primordial wisdom? Where did people look for meaning, before Christianity, before even science itself? From two and a half thousand years ago there's Socrates.

According to Socrates, what's most important in life is the welfare of the self. And that's entirely up to each of us. Only our own wrong actions can harm the self, only our own right actions benefit it. Other people can do us harm, but they can't harm our self unless we respond to their wrong-doing by doing wrong back. How we behave is what matters.

The key is practicing the virtues. In Socrates' day the virtues were courage, moderation, piety, wisdom and justice. Socrates wasn't big on piety, but he was a great believer in wisdom. If you use wisdom to study the other virtues you will want to live by them. His famous dialogues show him teasing people's problems apart to understand where true virtue lay. He believed the virtues lie in each of us, just needing to be brought out through questioning and discussion.

That places us right back where we are today, figuring out how to manage the self through questioning and discussion, in today's terms. There's no going back. We have to find our meaning in the present.

We also can't solve the problem of meaning by ignoring it. All that happens is, someone else defines the self for us.

We're likely to adopt meanings from the roles we play in life. One of these roles is seeing everything in terms of components, instead of wholes. That makes business and manufacturing very efficient, where machines can be plugged in and rearranged as needed. But we can start to see our selfs the same way, as bundles of skills and characteristics that can be individually plugged in and rearranged. We can lose our sense of being a whole.

Another meaning it's easy to adopt from our work is that roles and wishes can be divided up into items to plug in to schedules and calendars. It's tempting to divide our own lives up into items we plug in separately to fill our diaries and address books.

Can we find meaning in our biology?

Almost anything in our biology can be turned into meaning.

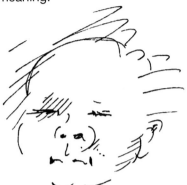

The kinds of people children see, or don't see, from the age of 6 months to a year and a half can affect who they'll regard as friends and strangers later in life. That's like the "imprinting" we see in animals.

If we value diversity we might turn this imprinting into a value about who should look after our children. Rather than wanting one person looking after them, someone like ourselves, we might instead want them looked after by a stream of different kinds of people.

That would be an example of how we can turn what we learn about our evolved nature into a new value.

But it isn't always obvious what meaning we should take from our biological nature. The meaning isn't just in our biology, it's in how we interpret it.

For example, biologically we're apes. But information about the great apes can be hard to apply as values to humans. Take the connection reported between males and female size and how many females a male lives with.

Should she care how much bigger than her they are?

At one extreme, when the males are very much larger than the females, there's only one adult male attached to the entire community of females. But if the two sexes are similar in size, as for Orangutans, the males and females tend to pair up one to one.

If you plot this as a graph and then look where we fall on it, our relative difference in size corresponds, I've read, to about one man to four women.

Now, the selection of data behind this finding could be biased, and personal judgment may affect where the curve is drawn. But let's assume we're persuaded that, as observation, it's sound. What do we do with such a finding?

Just walk away

We can do a number of things.

If we don't like the obvious implications of something like relative body size, we can, for example, ignore it, and simply celebrate other findings we do approve of. There's nothing wrong with that. We don't have to embrace something just because it's "natural." Society can easily compensate us for not doing what's "natural."

Or we could look at it for new kinds of meaning. We could apply game theory to it, for example. We might find that the words we first apply to the situation, such as "dominance" and "submission," aren't appropriate. Study of a tribe fairly new to Western civilization with a tradition of serial relationships similar to our marriages today found women benefiting from it just as much as, or even more than, men.

So even biology isn't a sure-fire route to meaning.

What's missing today is not just a new set of meanings, but a new system, a new principle to base meaning on.

What's plunged us into this restless search for new meaning? Isn't it science? Can we find our new meaning there?

I don't think we'll get much help from science. Science doesn't recognize the self, or consciousness. Given how little meaning science promises us, it's probably not surprising that people instead resort to assorted spiritualities. Many of them bear superficial resemblances to science — cosmic vibration, auras, rules of attraction. We look to science, but what we really want is something that recognizes we're conscious feeling selfs.

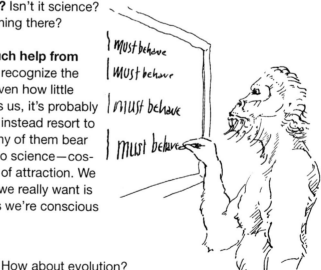

How about evolution?

CHAPTER 2

Meaning from Darwinism

You can divide human history and philosophy into two—before the discovery of evolution, and after.

That's how dramatic the discovery of evolution's been. It changes everything. It changes what everything means.

The idea of evolution first burst on the scene in 1844. It directly challenged mankind's most cherished beliefs, rousing a firestorm of controversy.

Here's what it said:

- **There's no such thing as destiny.** There's no ideal model of humanity ahead of us, beckoning us on.

- **The future's fundamentally unpredictable**, because future events arise through evolution, and there's no intelligence outside evolution entitled to hold forth about its direction.

- **We're not necessarily nature's favorites.** In evolution, there are no chosen people, there is no chosen species.

Compared to a belief in a loving God who watches over us and promises us Paradise, this is a terribly bleak system of beliefs.

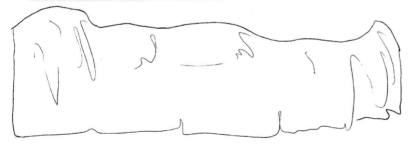

And this new system of belief only got bleaker when, 15 years later, Charles Darwin's "Origin of Species" at the same time nailed down the truth of evolution and proclaimed its mechanism to be natural selection, a purely physical process.

What meanings would that add to evolution's message?

We all want to be on the winning side.

Evolution's surely a winner, just look at what it's accomplished— it created us! Whatever we think evolution's winning strategy is, we'll be tempted to adopt it.

Let's look at the meanings found in evolution by modern Darwinism: natural selection, mutation, and adaptation to the environment.

Eugenics

In the early 1900's, evolutionists identified a meaning in natural selection they named "eugenics"—healthy heredity.

Eugenics meant applying "natural selection" to other people—those you thought weren't as well qualified to pass on their genes as you—by sterilizing them so they couldn't reproduce. The Nazis adopted this evolutionist doctrine to justify racial extermination.

Public outcry forced evolutionists to abandon the application of natural selection to people. But they just dropped it, they never explained why in principle it was wrong.

The logic behind eugenics in natural selection still applies.

Natural selection and population statistics

- In each generation of each species, its members are in competion to be among the few that survive to reproduce.

- The characteristics that most make for survival will concentrate in future generations, eventually defining a new species.

- These characeristics are due to genes. Evolution can be studied as changes in gene frequencies over time.

Will our genes be among those that survive to shape the future of our species? Natural selection says they will if they help us beat the competition. Darwin's point was, that selects for creatures better at coping with the environment, so over time evolution leads to greater adaptation to the environment.

But, that will select also for who's most aggressive, and promiscuous.

Want your genes to shape the future of the species? You can't do much about becoming better adapted to the environment. But you can make a better showing at sex and violence.

After reading Darwin's book, who would want to be a loser at natural selection? Sex and aggression got made into virtues first in Social Darwinism then in Freud's picture of the unconscious as a seething cauldron of violence and sexual passion. Freud's influence helped make those passions the primary plot-lines of popular drama. And why not? After all, isn't that what evolution says we're really about.

From natural selection we do get a path to greater self esteem—excelling in sex and violence. That's the primary meaning we're given by modern evolutionary theory.

Random mutation

What determines whether you're on evolution's winning team, worthy to pass on your genes?

Supposedly, what qualifies you to be a winner lies in accidents that strike your genes at random: getting zapped by cosmic rays, misaligned during reproduction, attacked by chemicals and viruses, and knocked out of kilter by thermal vibration.

This all amounts to one thing—accidental damage. Just occasionally, of course, some of that random damage could actually be an improvement on how we started out, making us more likely to survive.

In other words, as far as evolution is concerned, what's most important about us is accidents happening at random to our chromosomes. Our contribution to the further evolution of our species is limited to passively submitting to our genes being damaged, something we can do nothing about.

Lucky you!
You've just been
mutated!

Is that the most each of us can hope for; that some of the random damage our genes suffer has potential for making us more likely to survive? If so, then personal achievement is ultimately valueless.

What does that do for your self esteem? Not so much?

Adaptation to the environment

What is that? Becoming ever-more-closely molded around the pebbles and boulders of the environment? And once we've become perfect paper-thin impressions of those pebbles and boulders, what then? Even if living creatures start to form impressions of each other, how can they ever become more complex than the pebbles and boulders the first creatures molded themselves around?

Is that all we are? Is all creative thinking, whether we do it or evolution does it, just someone or something "adapting to its environment." Are eagles and parrots just dinosaurs "adapted" to air? Is inventing the internet just us "adapting" to electricity?

I don't think so. If evolution can make us, with our passion for learning and our ingenuity in coming up with self help, then whatever drives evolution consists of much more than just passive adaptation to the environment, in us and probably in all living creatures.

I don't see us getting much meaning from "adapting."

Why do evolutionists make such a big deal out of living creatures becoming ever-more adapted to the environment? Because that's the most you can expect from natural selection. Since that's all natural selection can do, they have to insist that's all evolution consists of, and all we should ask of it.

Being adapted to the environment is the most we can expect of our selfs: that's the third meaning we're taught by Darwinism.

Since Darwin's time, his concept of evolution has gone through some face-lifts. Have they helped make it more meaningful? Here are some additional meanings.

The selfish gene   Richard Dawkins popularized the notion that the most important players in evolution are our genes, some of which seem to have survived almost unchanged for billions of years. According to him, living creatures and species are merely how genes express themselves and compete among themselves for dominance in the gene pool.

Hello? Individual genes—individual small building blocks of the genome—use us as their playthings. Are we supposed to be inspired?

Gaia   Instead of the environment being a merciless agent of selection some biologists have transformed it into a benign "ecology." As it evolves, an ecology becomes home to a balanced set of interacting species that work together to stabilize it and make it comfortable. Grasses protect soil from erosion. Legumes fix nitrogen from the air and make it available to other plants. Those plants in turn provide fruits for animals to eat, which then carry the plants' seeds throughout their range. And so on. The whole earth, that ecology of ecologies, Gaia, is miraculously kept habitable through its creatures' combined interactions.

This is nice, but it is enough? Is life ultimately about gardening and keeping house?

We're nothing special   In response to the traditional story that we're the pinnacle of creation, the late Stephen J Gould insisted on a more politically correct story. Who were we to make ourselves the be-all and end-all of evolution? Evolution is mainly concerned with creating new kinds of bacteria. We're nothing more than a side-branch of a side-branch of a side-branch of living creation, and hence not important at all.

Value of diversity

No, no, put those scissors down!

Politically correct, but by itself surely not enough.

Darwinism doesn't provide us with sufficient meaning

CHAPTER 3

Evolutionary theories compared

We evolved.There's no doubt about that. There's overwhelming evidence to prove it.

But that doesn't tell you anything about natural selection. Evidence for evolution is not the same thing as evidence for natural selection.

Creatures being adapted to their environment isn't proof of natural selection either, living creatures are bound to be adapted to their environment no matter how they evolved, or they'd have gone extinct!

In fact, except for odd laboratory experiments there is no scientific evidence at all that natural selection is the primary mechanism of evolution.

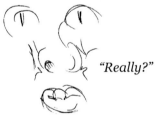

"Really?"

For over 200 years the pendulum's been swinging back and forth between two different explanations for evolution, Lamarckism and Darwinism. In our lifetime, from around 1940 to recently, Darwinism has reigned supreme. But now, once again, discoveries are tilting the balance back towards Lamarckism.

Darwinism says evolution is driven by the environment acting on living creatures from the outside—evolution is driven by physics.

Lamarckism says evolution is driven by something in living creatures, that directs evolution from the inside—evolution is driven by some kind of living intelligence.

What's likely to happen is a new theory will show both theories to be partly true, and partly false.

Something like that happened just a century ago. Do children inherit characteristics from their parents, or are they created anew? The science of genetics showed both were true, through the same genes being passed down in each generation but in different combinations, so each of us has a unique set of genes.

In these handbooks I show how Lamarckism, in the form of the intelligent genome theory, is a better guide to how to live.

When that new theory of evolution emerges, it will profoundly affect how we think about human nature, and what we expect of our selfs. Until then, we've our lives to lead, and a choice to make. Which of our existing theories—Darwinism or Lamarckism—gives us a better guide to how to live?

Darwinism as bad science

Not efficient enough

All that's special about living creatures, according to Darwinism, is that they reproduce themselves. They could be rocks reproducing themselves, or matchsticks, it wouldn't matter. All that's required is that they reproduce themselves almost exactly, with just occasional errors.

Then natural selection will weed out the errors that reduce viability, while letting through those errors that increase viability. Hey presto, an endless increase in viability!

Can it be so easy?

Not a self-reproducing rock

No, it can't. Many more mutations will be harmfull than beneficial, and natural selection is very inefficient. So, in each generation, many more damaging than beneficial errors will get through, leading to rapid extinction.

Why is Darwinism so popular? Because it can account for the creation of living creatures without God. But is that enough if it doesn't work?

Proof of evolution is not proof of natural selection

The intelligent genome as potential new science

We know conscious, thoughtful creatures able to make intelligent decision can exist, because we exist! Because we evolved, we know the process of evolution has involved creatures like that. Let's carry that idea to a logical conclusion, and expect conscious, thoughtful inteligence to be involved in the mechanism of evolution itself.

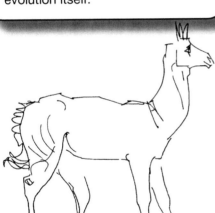

Take an animal like this deer. It's a whole. It passes through life stages from infancy to death, it has intelligence and feelings, it evolves, it reproduces. The intelligent genome theory maintains that wholeness, finding the intelligence of the genome manifested in every aspect of the creature's life.

Could mere molecules, such as our chromosomes, be intelligent? Yes, because:

- They're not isolated, they're parts of cells, which are very complex.

- We're intelligent, yet our brains are made of molecules.

So logically there's no reason why our chromosomes shouldn't work together, as our brain cells do, to support an intelligence.

We've nothing else in our world anything like the genome to compare it to, to tell us what it could be capable of.

Consider this: stretched out end to end, our chromosomes would stretch for three feet. The genome is a living creature three feet long! If you were to write the "letters" it's written in like ticker-tape, 8 letters to an inch, 100 to a foot, it would stretch from Los Angeles to New York City, and over the Atlantic Ocean to London.

And every time it divides to make a new cell, three foot of double-strand molecule splits down the middle, builds itself a new half, and all 3 billion "letters" are reproduced with almost no errors. Who's qualified to say what such a system is capable of? There's nothing else anything like it for scientists to draw conclusions from. You can't prove, scientifically, that the genome isn't intelligent.

From egg to adult to species

One way of looking at an animal's growth is, it's simply chemical. The plan of the growing animal is laid out in a complex pattern involving huge numbers of different chemicals all in precise concentrations. Each stage of growth directs the laying down of the even more complex pattern of chemicals needed for the next stage of growth.

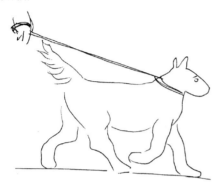

There's a problem with this: an animal like a puppy is a terrific stirrer of its own tissues. If it consisted one moment of a complex stew of chemicals all in precise concentrations you can bet that within two seconds it would start playing and romping and all those chemicals would get stirred together.

Something else must make each body plan follow the body plan of the previous stage of growth so precisely that the growing puppy ends up as the adult dog you expect of its breed.

And what's that? Believe it or not, your guess is as good as mine. Or as any scientist's. Because no one knows how it works. What little is known says, in the genome there's a complex set of specifications that somehow get communicated as a blueprint throughout the growing creature.

if that's true for development, won't something similar be true for evolution?

Problems with a science of an intelligent genome?

Throughout these handbooks I've talked about "the genome." But which genome?

All of them. All of them working together, somehow communicating with one another.

- all the chromosomes in a single cell,

- all instances of the genome in a living creature,

- all the genome's in the genome pool of the species,

- all the genomes in existence.

Yes, I have to suppose that genomes communicate with one another in some way we don't know about.

At what time scales can genomes act? Milliseconds, in cell metabolism, seconds in animal's dreams and behavior, weeks in development, years in aging, and aeons in evolution.

Do I really believe all that?
I believe nature acts as if that's all true. I believe science could be conducted on such a hypothesis. I believe useful observations would be made, and useful questions would be arrived at. But is it true? It's too soon to tell.

CHAPTER 4

Intelligent genome as meaning

Why do we all like ice cream? We wouldn't have come across sugar, cream or anything frozen in the environments early humans evolved in? We didn't adapt to ice cream.

Obviously we get meanings from other sources besides adaptation to the environment. In this chapter let's look for meanings in the idea of the intelligent genome.

"Boo-hoo! The genome doesn't love me!"

The genome probably cares about its creatures in general, since that's where it lives. But it probably doesn't care about those creatures individually, It creates more than enough of them and let's them be eaten by the creatures of other genomes.

So I don't think it has a soft spot for us individually. It equips us pretty well, then sets us loose. That's like us planning to release thousands of microscopic robots to explore some dangerous environment—we don't care about them individually, we want just one or two to survive long enough to report back.

"But I'm sure proud how well it equipped me."

The genome may not be much of a guardian angel. But it's a good creator. The genome gave each of us splendid capabilities, more than we'd expect from just being adapted to the environment, which is all we could expect from natural selection.

How well we're equipped is the meaning I wrote about in Handbook 1. That's a very important new meaning.

The distant prospect--
understanding the world better

Thinking is thoughts evolving, I suposed in Handbooks 1 and 2. If we could build that into science, the world would seem a much simpler place. All there'd be in the world would be matter the way today's science describes it, and thoughts evolving in consciousness. Anything that wasn't just matter, like a cloud, we'd describe in terms of processes of evolution.

- Living creatures would be the genome's thoughts expressed in matter,

- A bird's nest would be a bird's thoughts expressed in matter,.

- Technology would be our thoughts expressed in matter.

 Between the two, matter and evolution, we could account for all aspects of our lives and experiences.

- We could see animals and plants around us as having evolved.

- We could see our feelings and thoughts as having evolved.

- We could see our arts and our sciences as having evolved.

- We could see meaning itself as having evolved.

 A science combining material technologies and evolutionary processes could tackle a wider range of problems, from infectious diseases to contradictions within our own value systems.

 And being descended from apes wouldn't seem any kind of indignity. Nothing could be finer than being any kind of evolved creature. We'd reach out to all living creatures as our brothers.

Would they like that?

Consciousness—OK, that's still hard. It's something to do with evolving that we haven't quite figured out yet.

CHAPTER 5

Intelligent genome as mission

Can we communicate directly with the genome through our dreams?

In Handbook 1 I supposed our dreams are communications with the genome where it queries us and teaches us during sleeping consciousness. Ah, at last! I thought when this first occurred to me, I've found the key to what our dreams mean! I can communicate with the genome directly.

Some dreams seem like reports involving the new self. For example, I have dreams about driving, certainly not something the body originally evolved to do. In one recurring dream I'm driving a bus from about 200 feet up in the air, trying to turn the steering wheel to stop the main body of the bus, that I can see hundreds of feet below me, from crashing into other vehicles. But I suspect that's my original self reporting to the genome its anxiety about being made responsible for driving while consciousness is mainly taken up with new-self stuff?

Make what you want of this, **I've given up trying to communicate with the genome through my dreams.**

Can we find a new mission in our relationship with the genome?

Sins as mission? I don't think so.
The genome equipped us with healthy appetites. From watching television you'd think indulging them—what used to be called the sins of lust, gluttony, envy, malice and so on—are all the mission we need. Isn't that all Darwinism asks of us? Americans are even encouraged by their constitution to pursue "happiness."

But lust, gluttony, envy, and malice are merely ways the genome makes us maintain and reproduce ourselves. If they were our mission we wouldn't be satisfied by them so easily.

Pre-adapted for a new mission?
Besides those simple appetites, the genome equipped our ancestors with tools they used to create civilization. In the language of Darwinism, they came "pre-adapted" to invent civilization.

Since natural selection can't pre-adapt you for anything, Alfred Wallace concluded it couldn't be what drives human evolution. If he were alive today would he be able to pick out ways we're being pre-adapted for some new mission? Can we?

The genome's own mission?
OK, so the genome gives us the tools to invent civilization. But why? How does that help the genome achieve its own mission? Perhaps through the study of nature we'll identify that mission, and adopt it ourselves. What could be finer?

Pre-adapted to study material science?

Let's put these ideas together. What's the genome's goal likely to be and how could we participate in it?

Here are a few things we know:

- The genome is locked away in living cells, that's all it experiences directly.

- In addition, it gets what information it can, indirectly, from the fates and experiences of its creatures.

- It's become a master architect, chemist and engineer. It uses what it learns to make even more amazing living creatures. The more amazing creatures it creates, the more it can learn.

We also know it pre-adapted us to be capable of inventing civilization. It gave us hands and great intelligence. What else did it give us?

It gave us the ability to carry out material science.

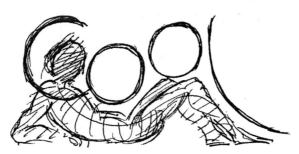

The genome is already a master of the use of materials. It designed the hemoglobin molecules around the properties of iron. It employs the properties of iodine in the thyroid. But it has no hands, no furnaces, no forges. We have all those. We make telescopes, spectroscopes. We've discovered electricity, nuclear power, quantum computers. The genome couldn't have access to all this know-how without us.

Is that our new mission? When our spacecraft send back photos of the solar system, do you glance at the those photos on the Internet? Perhaps, by passing those images through your attention, you're fulfilling the genome's deepest wish.

Is that mission enough?

Betty's mission

Let me introduce you to Betty. Betty's 57.
She's had all the children she's ever going to have. Now:

According to **Darwinism** she's

USE-LESS

because she can't have contribute more genes to the gene pool.
And:

WASHED UP

because natural selection can't lead to further development in people beyond childbearing age.

According to **intelligent genome theory** she's

USE-FULL

because the genome is still tracking her progress and experiences.
And:

IMPORTANT

because she's free to devote herself to the further evolution of the human species.

Mission of the aged

For the first time in world history there will soon be a huge population of "old" people, beyond child-bearing age. "Old age," from 55 to 90, for an increasing number of people will last as long as work-life, from 20 to 55. Together they make up a large proportion of all the human beings there have ever been. What impact could they have on the evolution of the species?

Will they make no impact at all, beyond by being grand-parents? Are they themselves, men and women, like Betty, useless? Are their lives now meaningless, because their genes are no longer subject to natural selection? Is this huge population on a biological scrap heap?

The plight of this huge population makes the choice between evolutionary theories significant. It isn't just academic. The self esteem of billions of the retired is at stake. As well, possibly, as the future of our species.

Being, and dying

These are two crucial areas where human elders could etch new strategies into the genome, through their experiences and decisions. They're highly qualified: they've wisdom; they've plenty of free time; they've fewer distractions. May they become leaders in the evolution of the human species?

Return of Lamarckism.
Recent research suggests experiences widespread in one generation can drive genetic changes in the generations following. This is reviving interest in Lamarckism, the alternative to Darwinism to which the intelligent genome theory is a contribution.

Could a kernel of scientific truth lie behind some of the world's religions? Have they glimpsed the work of genome intelligence but attributed it to an eternal, all-powerful and all-knowing being?

That wouldn't be far off. Evolution's not eternal but it's been going on for one third as long as the universe has existed. And it may not be all-powerful but it has transformed lifeless matter into creatures like us. What it isn't is all-knowing. It's made lots of mistakes, all those creatures that went extinct.

Religions help us form communities of belief and self help. Do we need a new "religion"? It's not easy to lead the good life alone. The quality of your experience of self depends a lot on the sense of self of the people around you. For a good life, you need to be among other people living the good life too. Self help needs to be shared.

Prelates of a future religion

Of course, anyone can claim anything they want to be the mission the genome sent us on, just as individual prophets read meaning into the Christian God. But unlike a god, the genome has to operate within clear limits. What we discover in nature around us, as well as in our own nature, will set limits to what we can conceive the genome's wishes to be, and what our mission is.

Let's leave religions to one side. What's needed is a better language, or "discourse," for exploring the human self. This could help us argue our way to the good life, as Socrates did using the ideas of his time.

But the choice of which theory of evolution we use as the basis of self help may be too important a question to leave to evolutionists. We may have to rein them in over this just as we did over eugenics.

A creation story for the rest of us

Have you heard of "the two cultures"? Jacob Bronowski came up with a neat explanation for what separates them. Bronowski met just about every important thinker in his day, so I believe he knows what he's talking about. He said this in 1967, but the division he's talking about has grown even deeper since then.

"The world is pretty well divided into people who are proud of being machines and people who are outraged at the thought of being machines."

(Reported in
"The Origins of Knowledge
and Imagination," 1978.)

Don't disagree with this man

Darwinism is the creation story of those who are proud of being machines. That's probably only one person in four, but they write most of the science books and are responsible for most teaching of evolution in school science classrooms.

Where's the creation story for the rest of us? Remember, there's no proof that Darwinism is what's behind the evolution of animals like us, over tens of millions of years. It's certainly true that we evolved, but that alone is not evidence for any particular mechanism.

The theory of natural selection is personal conviction posing as science. So is creationism. So is the theory of the intelligent genome. All three are creation stories supporting different views of how the universe is put together.

You're free to choose between them, and the selfs they lead to.

Evolutionary theory is too important
to leave to evolutionists

Tips on adopting a new self

Did you realize you could choose between selfs? You could join a spiritual cult, for example. You could become Christian and care for your soul. The Ancients made several selfs for people to choose between.

| Stoic | epicurian | Christian | Hedonist |

You could adopt a self based on science and become a robot. One choice you don't have is going back to some "natural" self people had hundreds of thousands of years ago, before civilization, before we had language. That self itself has evolved, through culture, into what we are today.

The Ancients based most of their selfs on philosophy. Modem selfs tend to be based on ideas drawn from religion or politics or science. In this book I introduced you to a new idea drawn from what we know about evolution, and a new self based on that new idea. I showed you how this new self works and ways to make it your own self. Actually, the self described in this book is quite like our traditional self. What's new is basing it on evolution. The benefit of that is, as more is discovered about evolution you can build more of your self upon it.

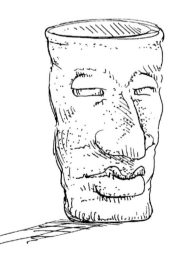

The concept of the genome thinking may lie outside today's science but there's no scientific evidence to contradict it. Today's young scientists have tremendous potential ahead of them for new thinking where evolution and consciousness converge.

Self as hobby
This book is meant to help you visualize the self and think and talk about it, almost as something tangible. Then you can work on it as a hobby, like pottery or woodwork, a lifelong pastime. Read the book again and you'll find lots of examples.

Take back your attention

Key to this project is taking control of your attention. All around us there are people trying to grab our attention and harness our self to their ends. We're constantly in danger of being seduced by advertising, music, free gifts, sexual temptation, food treats, it's an endless barrage.

We're like Odysseus—he had himself lashed to the mast of his ship and ordered his crew to sail in the opposite direction from where he pointed, towards the isle of the Sirens and their irresistible singing. By having them sail in the opposite direction is how he escaped shipwreck. If we're to avoid having our self exploited for other people's benefit we have to be both Odysseus and his crew, navigating away from easy temptation and distraction. If you value your self it's worth always asking, can I do more with my self than they can?

Call to a greater self

It's amazing but true—we do have control over our self. I think that is how the giants of the Renaissance thought about their selfs. No challenge seemed too great. Then over time the concept of self got smaller and smaller. People out to hijack your attention tell you it's your duty to consume the titillating news and mindless entertainment they offer. It's not your duty. Your duty is to a higher authority, the process of evolution that gave you your amazing self.

Segregate the self from science

How about brain science? Can you learn how the self works from biochemistry or brain anatomy? No. You already know how the brain works, you experience it as consciousness. That's what the brain is designed to do, and science can't tell you anything more about that than you can experience from the inside.

The power of amazement

Can we measure our success? I think we can, through our self respect. That's the key measure of self improvement. And what's our best source of self respect? I believe it's recognizing what we have in common with what's most amazing around us. It's a paradox we live with second by second—what's most extraordinary around us is also what's most common, that we're almost bound to take for granted—plants, trees, birds, caterpillars, flies, houseplants, and of course, each other.

It's a constant challenge to maintain the appropriate amazement. But unless we do we risk overlooking where the greatest value in life lies. We can realize that value by channeling our amazement into what we expect of our self, our own self respect.

Forget Charles Darwin, escape the clutch of grubby Victorian materialism, let yourself imagine how wonderful the process of evolution must be, and feel joy at knowing you embody that same process in your own self.

If you decide to adopt an inteligent-genome self, don't be surprised if you meet hostility. Any retreat from Darwinism angers some people, and they may become abusive. What's going on?

Some people have made Darwinism the foundation of their self. Criticism of Darwinism is an attack on everything they hold most dear. They tend to defend themselves without respect for courtesy. They're even proud of following in a tradition of "Darwin's bulldogs." They shouldn't be.

When you become involved in evolutionary theory, you'll find it's a jungle out there. But remember, you're entitled to fight back in self defense. Stand up for what you believe.

Other titles published by

EVOLVED SELF PUBLISHING

Save Our Selves from Science

"Shaun Johnston raises many fascinating questions, asking how it is that many scientists seem to find it so embarrassingly difficult to think about any sort of consciousness, especially their own, that they'd rather say it isn't there?... But they badly need to be pressed to roll up their sleeves and face it directly. So, all good wishes to Johnston as he pesters them to get over their scruples!"

> **Mary Midgley**, Gifford Lecture 1989-90, *Science As Salvation* and author of *Evolution as a Religion: Strange Hopes and Stranger Fears*.

"In *Save Our Selves from Science Gone Wrong*, Shaun Johnston presents selectionism as the science that has gone wrong, corrupting biology as well as pertinent aspects of sociology, philosophy, and the popular media. Such a strong voice deserves attention. Responding to the question, 'What do you put in its place?', Johnston begins at the top, with the consciousness of the individual self."

> **Robert G. B. Reid**, Emeritus Professor of Biology at the University of Victoria British Columbia, and author of *Evolutionary Theory: The Unfinished Synthesis* and *Biological Emergences: Evolution by Natural Experiment*.

164 pages, 5 1/2 x 8 1/2. Paperback. USA $14.95. ISBN 0-9779470-2-5. Available through Amazon.

Me and The Genies

Cynical TV executive Henry Lazaard ("Lizard") is made manager of beautiful Sung-Tin Chi, Chinese scriptwriter for a children's cartoon series. Turns out, Sung-Tin's inspiration is evolution, specifically a mysterious document called "Beths Book." Follow their romance as Henry works to sabotage Sung-Tin's attempt to reform him. Along the way Sung-Tin reveals a plan for world domination that hangs on a clash between two concepts of the self, and explains evolution's role in forming them.

A quick-read introduction for teachers and school board members to the parties and issues involved in the controversy over teaching evolution in the classroom.

220 pages, 5 1/2 x 8 1/2. Paperback. USA $14.95.

ISBN 0-9779470-0-9. Available through Amazon.

Father, in a Far Distant Time I Find You

It is 6991AD. Drawing on his father's wisdom about our time and our future, student Gregory Dumont shows us human nature being transformed by successive stages in evolutionary theory during a 2000-year-long "Age of World Figures" starting about 1000 years in our future.

Combining a broad historical sensibility with respect for the discipline of scientific discourse, "Father..." reveals the implications for human nature of evolutionary theory over the past two centuries, readying us to assess the implications of steps to come. The take-home message—evolutionary theory shapes us as much as we shape it. Fine addition to the multi-disciplinary study of evolution.

202 pages, 5 1/2 x 8 1/2. Paperback. USA $21.95.

ISBN 0-9779470-1-7. Available through Amazon.

Breinigsville, PA USA
30 April 2010
237116BV00004B/1/P